JAMES

AND THE

HUMAN GENOME: CLONE WARS

GAIL E. DAVIES

Science
LEARNING CENTRES

For James and Charlie

The author would like to thank the following:
The Wellcome Trust for their funding;
Michael Reiss, Angela Hall and Marilyn Watts for their support;
and all the teachers and pupils who took part in the project.

First published in Great Britain in 2007 by Science Learning Centre
London

A CIP catalogue record of this book is available from the British Library

ISBN: 978-0-9555723-0-2

Designed by Paul Barrett
Production services by Book Production Consultants Ltd
Printed and bound in Great Britain by William Clowes Ltd, Beccles, Suffolk

This book is divided into two sections. The first section, Part 1, is a story detailing the scientific background to cloning. The story is fictional but the science is real. The second section, Part 2, is a science fiction story. This uses scientific ideas but is not meant to be true science.

PART 1

JAMES AND THE HUMAN GENOME

PART 2

CLONE WARS: OUR STORY

PART 1

JAMES AND THE HUMAN GENOME

1

A CLONE OF AN IDEA

Let me introduce myself. My name is James and I have a gross younger brother called Charlie. The family situation sound familiar? I enjoy school (for the benefit of any of my teachers reading this, who might misguidedly think this is a serious science book). Well, to be honest, I do sometimes. I have to say the lunches are great and the odd lesson has its merits. Principally though, it keeps me out of the family clutches, which is not a bad thing, especially when they involve Charlie.

I always fancied myself as a mad scientist. That was after the vet stage (Mum wouldn't allow pets into the house, so early training was out), and the idea of tinkering around a laboratory with the odd explosion sounded pretty cool. Mum and Dad were not convinced of the career choice, especially after the homemade fireworks incident, and said that I watched too much television.

Why did I ever mention I liked science? Ever since then, Dad has been harping back to his "days" as a chemist. He was always going on anyway about research being nothing like in the movies, and how chemistry wasn't just about explosions, it was a serious science. Clearly, in his reality check, he forgot that he had amused me with tales of student pranks involving radioactive sources. How responsible is that!

Still, these days Dad conformed to being a normal member of the rat race and disappeared off to work at the crack of dawn. Not high on the excitement scale.

Mum, on the other hand, is a bit more interesting. She is a scientist, and what's more, a geneticist. That's cool. No more thoughts of exploding labs and chemistry for me; that idea faded. A mere blip in my childhood fantasies. Genetics was the future: I had heard that somewhere, and I don't think it was from Mum. Now I would have my chance to create the perfect super-being. I could make a double, clone myself. I knew it was possible, I had seen it in the headlines of Dad's paper. Why was I interested? Why did I care? Well, this was the perfect project for the schools summer science competition. I knew the nerdy clique were entering, the teachers were already fawning over their a-m-a-z-i-n-g ideas. I would show those doubters in the science department.

"James needs to focus more to fulfil his potential."

"His organisational skills and concentration need some attention."

Just the sort of report comments that give you so much grief from the parents. Well, prepare to be amazed by my focus and determination. You never know, I might even win. That would be a turn-up for the books. There was one minor niggling thing: I had to find out how to clone. This was going to be the boring bit. I never did like reading the instructions of how to master any new computer game, just have a go, bound to get the hang of it eventually. Alternatively, you could ask someone who already knows how, ask a friend.

That was it: I could ask Mum. Well, I had to be careful, I couldn't just blurt out, "Hey, Mum, how do I go about cloning someone?" I'm sure she would disapprove on moral grounds. Adults always seem to get hung up on doing the right thing.

I had to be subtler than that, employ the smooth negoti-ating skills that I was honing to perfection. I had to feign genuine interest in genetics – well it was sort of genuine – as a means to an end. I did want to win the competition. Okay, not just to prove everyone wrong, there was the small matter of the prize money, not to be sniffed at. I quite fancied the new games console coming out. Still, back to the task in hand, I had to ask the right questions without rousing suspicion. Now this could be the difficult bit as I was starting from a below-zero baseline. I didn't know the first thing about genetics. I pondered on the problem for several days. I checked the web, and bizarrely came across several sets of instructions ranging from cloning yourself to cloning your pet. At first I was a little disheartened, my project had already been done. Then, on closer inspection, even I could tell they were the incoherent ramblings of nutcases. I got so desperate I even contemplated taking books out of the library, but sadly when I asked the librarian, she said that there wasn't a "How to Clone" Manual or anything of the kind. I was getting nowhere, and besides, as I said before, trawling for information could be tedious. To help me in this personal quest, my very own holy grail, I decided that I needed a muse and a confidante. Well, there was my good friend Katie next door. She was slightly older, much bigger, and equally crazy. She would do. It would be easier with two of us gleaning information. Maybe Mum would be less suspicious, after all Katie had always said that she wanted to be a doctor. Okay, so cloning perhaps isn't the first class on the agenda at medical school, but I wouldn't mind taking bets that it might be in the practical classes by the time Katie gets there.

IN THE BEGINNING: FIRST THERE WERE TWO AND THEN THERE WERE FOUR

" In the beginning God made Adam and Eve," or so the story goes, but it all went horribly wrong with the snake. I was not going to let anything go wrong with my plans. Nothing could be left to chance. I had approached Katie with the idea, and she had been on for it. I have a feeling that she was imagining a slave at her beck and call, attractive I had to admit, but surely that was what parents were for. Provided you trained them well. I, on the other hand, had grander plans. I could see the headlines now: "Super-being created by boy genius!"; "The start of a new super-race." In my darker moments I saw the flip side with the headline, "A new Frankenstein is born." A thought then went through my head: can clones be born? The technicalities were starting to raise their ugly heads. Maybe I should clone Charlie: go for monster creation straight off. He was certainly better starting material for that. Still, I fancied the idea of creating a super-being. I guess the nitty gritty of who to clone could be dealt with at a later stage. First things first, Katie and I had to get to grips with the basics. What was this DNA stuff that Mum kept going on about? Calling it deoxyribonucleic acid was about as useful as Shakespeare.

We had to get this stuff into plain and simple English. Okay, I appreciate to those of us still struggling with formidable English grammar it isn't always plain and simple, but let's face it, these doctors and scientists had the monopoly on incomprehensible language.

Much to my disgust, Katie suggested that we do some background work, find out some of the basics. I could see her point, that it would help to know what questions to ask. I happily conceded, and left Katie to it. We met up a few days later. She confessed that it wasn't that easy. There was a lot mentioned about helices and building blocks of life, but very little that made sense or was of use. This could be more difficult than we first imagined. Little were we to realise that this was the understatement of the year, if not century. We could see by now that if we were ever to complete this task we needed recruits.

I approached Ed at school the next day. I gave him the low-down in a quiet corner of the playground. After all, we didn't want the nerdy crew to get a whiff of any competition at this early stage. Ed could see the potential for greater things, commercial exploitation, a man after my own heart. He was already planning populating his dream theme park with clones. Move over Mickey Mouse.

The next recruit was Luke. I had to wait until he came round after school one day, as he was now a captive of the local boys' Catholic school. I knew that Luke would be interested but he had the potential of being a conscientious objector, after all he was a vegetarian. Still, it was always useful to have someone thinking about the ethics and morality of scientific research. I carefully explained the plan to Luke, saying that no animals would be hurt and after all it was humans that we wanted to clone. He was relaxed. I felt now that we had reached our critical mass. First we were two and now we were four. This was a good number. Later on in my school career I was to realise the significance of doubling and cell growth.

All we had to do now was work out a strategy for gathering the data needed. The holidays were looming so we would soon be able to dedicate our valuable time without the interruption of school work. The schools science competition was perfect cover, with the added incentive of perhaps winning. Potential fame and fortune aside, it would be worth it to wipe the smug smiles off the nerds' faces. With that thought in mind, the scientific dream team was assembled. Mum would be delighted that we had decided to enter the competition, if not a little surprised. We had to hope that she didn't question our motive, or us, too carefully. The less she knew the better.

LESSON ONE – CELLS AND GENES

There were no problems. Mum fell for it hook, line and sinker. But she did want to know what exactly our project was on?

"Science," said Luke, suitably vague.

"Yes, but that is rather a large topic. Don't you think you ought to narrow it down a little?" asked Mum.

"We thought that we would create our very own genetics experiment," said Ed.

"What were you thinking of? Making Frankenstein, a few designer babies perhaps?" laughed Mum.

I could tell she wasn't taking us too seriously or had she now added mind-reading to her skills? We had to tread carefully, and operate on a strictly need-to-know basis.

We managed to convince Mum that the project would take shape once we had got to grips with the basics. She agreed to help us and that was how our series of informal genetics classes started.

Mum said that genetics could explain why some things are the same and why some things are different, such as why people from the same family look alike and those from other families look different. She looked at me and said that I had the classic Davison ears. True, if you looked at family photos they were quite distinctive. There was a great one of Great-Grandad, Grandad, Dad and myself, nicely illuminated from the window behind. You could spot those ears anywhere. Katie looked different from us, not only because she was from a different family, but also because she was Chinese. This meant that her genes came from a whole different starting point to others in the United Kingdom, in fact a different gene pool. Mum said not to worry about this for now. She said that first we needed to consider cells. This is what she told us.

Cells

These are the real building blocks, house bricks if you like, of the body. Our entire body is made up of cells. These are tiny and can only be seen with a microscope. Obviously, we are not made of just one type of cell or we would all be huge blobs. We have different types of cells that can do different things, such as those which make up our skin, our heart, and our bones, but each cell is based on the same simple model and has the same bits inside. If you use a super-powerful electron microscope you can see what is inside. Just like we have organs inside our body, the cell has its own organs, called organelles. The one central to genetics is the **Nucleus**.

Nucleus

This is the control centre of the cell, the headquarters where all the decisions are made. This has the instructions to tell the cell what to do and what to become. Should it be a bone cell or a skin cell? Now, it can't do whatever it likes; there are very detailed instructions in the nucleus of each cell. These instructions are contained in something called **DNA**. Which stands for the unpronounceable deoxyribonucleic acid. No wonder it is called DNA.

Chromosomes, DNA and Genes

Even the simplest things are never as simple as they seem. There is always that next level of complexity. Okay, so the DNA carries all the instructions, and there are a whole lot of them. Having one long list floating around is untidy and takes up too much space, so what do you do? You pack the DNA up tightly into separate "bundles" which are called **chromosomes**. But there is so much DNA that you need 46 bundles, which are arranged in 23 pairs. All our genetic information is contained in 46 chromosomes, the information that gives me the Davison ears and makes Katie look Chinese. So where do these genes fit in, the genes that everyone keeps talking about? The DNA is a list of instructions, telling each cell what to do and ultimately making us what and who we are. Like any list of instructions there are lots of bits that don't really tell you anything, or it's not possible to work out what it's trying to tell you. DNA is just the same, and there are large bits of it that tell us nothing (or perhaps scientists haven't been clever enough yet to work out what it says): this is junk DNA. Then there are small bits of the DNA, very specialised bits of instructions, that do something. These bits are called **genes**. While most of the DNA is junk, there are 20,000–25,000 genes in a human. Some of these genes will decide what eye colour and hair colour we each have. To think that we need that number of genes to make a person. That is seriously complicated. What is even scarier is that a worm has around 18,000 genes, many of which are related to ours, and a plant has about 26,000 genes. So Charlie really could be a lower form of life after all.

In an attempt to try and make sense of the information that Mum was spurting out, I jotted down a quick diagram (James' Jottings 1). So, if I had it right, we had a large number of genes in our DNA which made us look like we do, and made us ourselves and nobody else. What I didn't understand was how come we were all different? Shouldn't we all have the same instructions to make us humans?

Mum was marginally impressed by the question, but tried not to show it.

James' Jottings 1

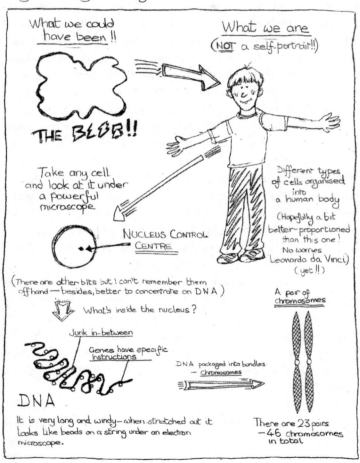

"Yes, we do all have the same fundamental instructions, such as we need a heart, lungs, feet and so on. But we don't have exactly the same DNA, or we would all be the same. We need variations, little changes or differences, in the DNA to make us individuals. Obviously, not such big differences that we can't make our vital organs, but a bit like the instructions for making a car. They all have four wheels and work on the same principle of a combustion engine. But there are still lots of different makes and models. This could be considered the same as humans. After all we come in different races and families. You can spot the similarities and differences, but like cars are all cars, we are all humans."

Mum stopped at that point, conceding that we had taken in enough for one day and that she would fill us in on the details another time. I couldn't wait! – though, sarcasm aside, I did feel I had learnt something and it was potentially interesting. Cloning here we come.

DINOSAUR BONES IN MY PACKED LUNCH

Mum got carried away. She was so convinced of our enthusiasm for science that she thought she would reward us with a trip to the Natural History Museum — her idea of a reward, not ours. Personally I thought she was insane taking the four of us along with Charlie for an educational day out.

The tube train was uneventful. Mum virtually frog-marched us through the subway at South Kensington; a minor embarrassment, not having been made to walk in a crocodile since Nursery. At last we were climbing the stone steps to the entrance and emerged through the barrier and into the large open hall.

"What a splendid building," Mum crooned, looking around. Why did she always say that every time we came here?

Having deposited coats and things, we sat squashed together on a bench while Mum dished out snacks and made unhelpful suggestions as to what to do next. A round of crisps and juice were readily demolished and that was it, the troops were heading for the dinosaur exhibition. Charlie, fired up on artificial stimulants and additives, was leading the way.

"I think that it is very important from a genetic point of view, the evolution of the dinosaurs," said Mum.

"I like the carnivores best," shouted Charlie, bloodthirsty as ever.

"I like the Stegosaurus, with his brain the size of a walnut," laughed Luke.

"Hey, he's also a vegetarian like you," I pointed out.

"So do all vegetarians have a walnut brain?" said Charlie, predictably.

"Now Charlie, don't be silly," said Mum, who had been carefully explaining something to Katie. Maybe Katie was using this as an opportunity to gain some vital information for the clone project, code name Superman. (Katie had taken some issue with this on the grounds that we might clone Superwoman. However, I carefully pointed out that it was just a term, after all we were all humans, not hu-man and hu-woman. She was not convinced, but heavily out-numbered.)

The dinosaurs were impressive as usual. As we were heading into the dark, the territory of the robotic dinosaur, I was reminded of Jurassic Park. Now that was about cloning dinosaurs. How did they do that? If only I could remember the film. Ed might remember, he was a man for detail.

"Ed, do you remember how the dinosaurs were made in Jurassic Park?"

"Wasn't it all computer stuff?" ventured Ed.

"No, not how the film was made, you know, the actual science," I said.

"Oh, that. It was from some blood-sucking insect that they found preserved in amber, I think," said Ed, coming up with the goods having now engaged his brain.

"That's it, a mosquito from the time of the dinosaurs trapped in amber. But how do you get from that to a huge dinosaur?" I said, looking back at the dinosaur skeletons. I must remember to ask Mum about that.

I wasn't to get the chance just then. There was a horrendous cry, and a lot of commotion up ahead. Ed and I looked at each other. Instinctively I knew Charlie was involved. We ran around the corner, closely followed by Mum and Katie. There we could see Charlie in the middle of the exhibit. The robotic dinosaur was turning its head and roaring as Charlie was scrabbling around on the floor trying to get back out without being noticed. Luke, almost having a seizure laughing, was standing at the edge. Apparently, Luke had dared Charlie to venture in and pick up one of the dinosaur eggs. He had no problem getting in, but getting out was proving more difficult. The shriek of Mum's voice provided the extra motivation that he needed. What was it with Charlie and dinosaurs? I recalled having to leave Stockholm museum when he climbed a skeleton there some years back.

The rest of the day went off uneventfully and at last we were sat on the train heading home, and I remembered my question.

"Mum, how did they make the dinosaurs in Jurassic Park?"

"Wasn't it some fancy computer graphics?" she replied absent-mindedly.

"*OHHH.*" Ed and I groaned collectively.

"No," I persevered. "The mosquito and amber and stuff, how does that all work?"

"Well, it doesn't really, because it would be impossible." Mum paused, sensing that we weren't really in the mood for a scientific lecture on the technicalities of whether this was true science or not. "Okay," she went on, "the mosquito was supposed to have been around at the time of the dinosaurs and had just fed, sucking some blood from one of them. It was then trapped in some tree sap which became the amber. Basically, the mosquito was preserved for many many years with a stomach-full of dinosaur blood." Mum stopped there, scouring my face for any signs of comprehension.

"Yes, but how were they supposed to get a dinosaur from dinosaur blood?" I asked.

"That's where genetics comes in. It is possible to get DNA from blood. You remember I told you about cells, and the nucleus containing DNA? Well, although the red blood cells don't have a nucleus, the white blood cells do, and so they contain DNA. It is relatively easy to get the DNA from them, but you only get lots of DNA if you have lots of blood." She paused for breath.

"But you wouldn't have a lot of dinosaur blood in a mosquito's stomach, would you?" asked Ed.

"No, that's right. You then need special ways of amplifying the DNA, increasing the amount you have. I know that's not very clear, but say if you had a small amount of blood, so you only got a small amount of DNA, you wouldn't be able to do much with it, like having one small piece of string. So, what we can do in the laboratory is to multiply the DNA, increase the amount using a special method so that you get lots of pieces of the same string, and that means you have more DNA to work with."

"So how were they supposed to get the dinosaur by having some of its DNA?" asked Katie.

I was with Katie on this one. It was a big leap from a scrap of DNA to a whole huge dinosaur.

"Well, you actually need all of the DNA, all of the instructions, not just a scrap of it. Still, you must remember it is only a film, so not really feasible, although the theory is based on real science. What was supposed to have happened was that a large amount of dinosaur DNA was extracted, and was sequenced. Before you ask I'll tell you what that means. Sequencing is reading the DNA. We talked about the DNA containing genes and junk, but what I didn't mention was that there is another level, the actual language of the genes, a code. This is the genetic code, a sort of machine code or computer code of the instructions." Mum paused. She could tell by the expression on our faces that she had totally lost us in her gobbledegook. She rummaged around in the bottomless pit of her bag and pulled out some paper and a pen. Why did she always carry around so many bits and pieces? She furiously began drawing, stopped, and then once again tried to explain. The words **Genetic Code** stood out from the paper.

"The DNA in our genes has the information that builds a human and allows it to function, walk, talk, digest food and much more. It is all very complicated, but really what needs to happen is that the DNA carries a code, a language that the cells can use, and that tells them what to do. Firstly though, we need to think about what we are made of. Putting it simply, we are one big lump of protein and water. It is the protein that builds us. Our skin, hair, heart, eyes are all made of different types of protein. Also, the bits that make us work, the juices digesting our food, the passing of messages in our brain so that we walk and talk, are all made up of specialised proteins."

Okay, so I get the message. I am just one great lump of protein, but a very sophisticated one. What was the difference between that lump of cheese (lots of protein in cheese) that Mum kept trying to persuade me to eat and, say, Charlie? Well, on some days I think it was difficult to tell. As far as I could see, he was more complicated, made of lots of different proteins, and living.

"So, where does the protein come from?" I asked.

"Well," Mum replied, "the DNA contains a code, a series of secret coded messages, that give the cells the instructions about which proteins to make. Surprisingly, this code, the genetic code, is made of only four things. These four things are actually chemicals, but don't worry about what these are as we always write them down as four letters,

AGCT. These four letters are then used in a set way (the genetic code has rules just like any secret code or language) to make proteins. One rule is that they have to be grouped into threes, triplets, to be read by the cell, a bit like arranging the alphabet in groups to make words."

Mind you, I thought, with just four letters and only three-letter words it would be a lot quicker to learn this language rather than English, with its 26 letters and ridiculously long words. These cells were clearly sensible when they were thinking of writing their own language.

"So if I have it straight," I said, "it's the DNA that contains the genes, that carry the code to make the proteins that build us." It all sounded rather like the old woman who swallowed a fly. I could almost imagine my DNA wriggling and tickling inside me.

By now we pleaded that we understood that DNA was made of a specific code of "letters" that told the cells what to build and do. Mum then explained that scientists were able to look at the DNA and read the coded message, like a spy deciphering coded messages. I studied Mum's sketches (Mum's Jottings 1).

"So, back to the film, using the dinosaur DNA that had come from the blood in the mosquito, the scientists were able to read the DNA, the coded instructions for making a dinosaur?" I hesitated, getting my thoughts together. This really was the same as the old woman who swallowed a fly. I don't know why she swallowed a fly…let alone how you make a dinosaur.

"In theory, that is the idea," said Mum.

"Neat," said Ed.

"However, it is not quite that easy, even in a film. You wouldn't expect to get the whole of the dinosaur's DNA, all the instructions in one piece. It would be broken into bits and some chunks would be missing. Still, using the

Mum's Jottings 1

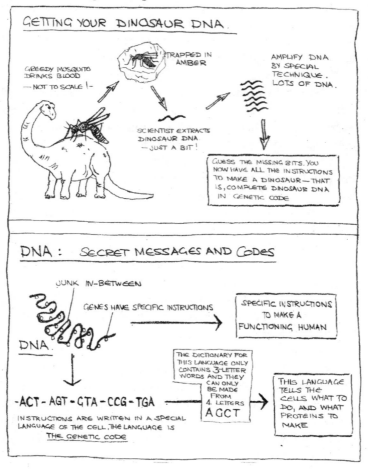

GETTING YOUR DINOSAUR DNA

GREEDY MOSQUITO DRINKS BLOOD — NOT TO SCALE !—

TRAPPED IN AMBER

AMPLIFY DNA BY SPECIAL TECHNIQUE. LOTS OF DNA.

SCIENTIST EXTRACTS DINOSAUR DNA — JUST A BIT!

GUESS THE MISSING BITS. YOU NOW HAVE ALL THE INSTRUCTIONS TO MAKE A DINOSAUR — THAT IS, COMPLETE DINOSAUR DNA IN GENETIC CODE

DNA : SECRET MESSAGES AND CODES

JUNK IN-BETWEEN

GENES HAVE SPECIFIC INSTRUCTIONS

SPECIFIC INSTRUCTIONS TO MAKE A FUNCTIONING HUMAN

DNA

-ACT- AGT- GTA- CCG- TGA

INSTRUCTIONS ARE WRITTEN IN A SPECIAL LANGUAGE OF THE CELL. THE LANGUAGE IS THE GENETIC CODE

THE DICTIONARY FOR THIS LANGUAGE ONLY CONTAINS 3-LETTER WORDS AND THEY CAN ONLY BE MADE FROM 4 LETTERS A G C T

THIS LANGUAGE TELLS THE CELLS WHAT TO DO, AND WHAT PROTEINS TO MAKE

knowledge of genes and DNA sequenced from other animals, it would theoretically be possible to put the bits into the right order, and then perhaps guess the bits you're missing. A sort of huge dinosaur jigsaw."

"That could be disastrous if you guess the wrong bit, you could end up with a really weird dinosaur," laughed Luke.

"It might even die," said Charlie with relish.

"You're both right, but the other thing to remember is that just because you have the DNA sequence, the dinosaur instructions if you like, it is a big jump to actually making the dinosaur. It is not quite like cookery, but it does have its similarities. You can't just throw in the list of ingredients and expect a fantastic meal to appear. There are steps in between, and it is just the same with the dinosaur. There are particular ways of making the whole DNA sequence into a real dinosaur. Remember, dinosaurs were generally egg layers. So you would need to get yourself a dinosaur egg, that you would empty of its DNA and then put into it the DNA you have to make your dinosaur. This is where it gets even less likely, as we don't have any viable dinosaur eggs around. However, once you have done that, put your DNA instructions into an egg, you can effectively grow your own dinosaur. This whole process is called cloning, making a copy." Mum paused, looking at us anxiously. "I am sure that I have lost all of you at this point. I did say it was complicated. Anyway, all you need to remember is that if we did manage to get all of the DNA, and it does have to be all of it, that DNA can be used to make a copy of the creature that it came from. It is not very easy but it is possible in theory, if not in practice." Mum sat back in her seat and closed her eyes.

It didn't matter that this was the stuff of fiction, as far as I was concerned it was theoretically possible to clone a dinosaur. I absent-mindedly doodled away (James' Jottings 2). Surely then it had to be easier to clone a human. Despite all this gobbledegook, we were getting there. The great experiment would take place before the end of the holidays. I was sure of it. I felt it in my bones. As I was happily daydreaming of great scientific acclaim and fortune, Charlie sidled up to me.

James' Jottings 2

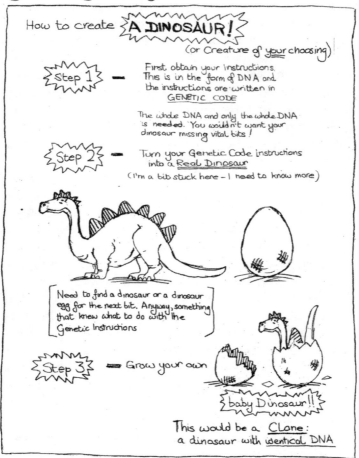

"Want to see what I've got?" he whispered, clutching something close to himself under his sweatshirt. He seemed to be nervously looking around, checking that Mum was still dozing.

"What is it?" I asked in a bored tone.

"A real dinosaur bone. I picked it up when I climbed into the dinosaur pit."

"Don't be ridiculous," I said, trying to hide my excitement. This could be our chance to clone a dinosaur. Couldn't archaeologists get DNA from bones or something? Charlie pulled out a rather large bone. He certainly hadn't found that in his packed lunch. The others gathered round and examined the bone.

"Can't be," said Katie.

"Well, he did get it from inside the exhibit, it might be real," said Luke.

I must say it was a great story, but we really had no way of proving that the bone was from a dinosaur. We could hardly take it back and ask one of the curators. It looked and felt like bone, and it certainly wasn't plastic. We never did find out whether it was an oversized chicken bone or a real dinosaur bone. Charlie insisted that it was real and kept the bone safe in his secret drawer. He may still have it.

LESSON TWO – CREATING AN INDIVIDUAL

Mum decided that we needed to get to grips with the basics of inheritance; why did we look like our families, and why can you often spot brothers and sisters without first knowing that they are related?

So the four of us were sat with Mum around the table, looking longingly at Charlie and his friend Richard playing in the garden. Well, it was all in the interests of science, for the greater good of mankind. Just imagine how proud our parents would be when they discovered that we had cloned the first human! I was lost again in my daydreams. There we were, being thanked by the Prime Minister for our contribution to science. Mum and Dad were crying buckets, saying that they had never appreciated how much of a genius I was. My teachers were busy backtracking to say that they knew I had the potential. Back to reality, Katie was kicking me under the table, and Luke and Ed were ploughing their way through the plate of biscuits. If I wasn't careful there would be none left, and everyone knows that you can't think on an empty stomach. A starving artist perhaps, but definitely not a starving scientist…not in my book. Starvation might be good for creativity but not for creation.

23 pairs of chromosomes are needed for a human

"Okay," Mum said. She started by reminding us that we humans had our DNA arranged into 23 pairs of chromosomes. They consisted of **chromosomes 1 to 22**, which were numbered roughly in size order from the biggest to the smallest.

"But that's only 22. I thought you said there were 23 pairs?" queried Katie.

She was absolutely right, why wasn't there a number 23? Mum explained that the last pair of chromosomes were different and were called the **X and Y chromosomes**.

"That's not a pair, if they are X and Y," said Ed.

"Do you get two Xs as a pair and two Ys?" I asked.

"And what about if you had an X and a Y together?" asked Luke.

"If you have all those combinations to make a pair, XX, XY and YY, then surely that would mean we could have different sets of chromosomes, and so we can't all be the same?" asked Katie looking very puzzled.

Mum laughed, and said that we were all sort of right.

"Okay, let's say that there are different sets, or combinations, of X and Y. Can you get different types of humans?" Mum asked.

We all looked at each other. I could only think of Charlie and the rest of the human species, but I was sure it would take more than a variation in X and Y chromosomes to make him so different. Then the penny dropped.

"Boys and girls are different," I said triumphantly. They certainly were.

Mum then explained that only two combinations were possible. Two X chromosomes **(XX) as a pair to make a girl** and an X and a Y chromosome together **(XY) as a pair to make a boy**. She then pulled out our box of crayons and did a quick sketch to show us (Mum's Jottings 2a and 2b). So far so good. But what I wanted to know was where did one get these chromosomes from? You clearly didn't go out and buy your set of chromosomes and then create your baby, or

Mum's Jottings 2a : A Boy's Chromosomes

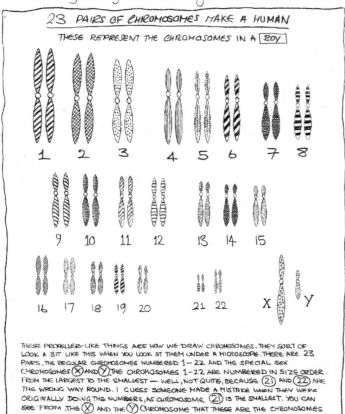

23 PAIRS OF CHROMOSOMES MAKE A HUMAN

THESE REPRESENT THE CHROMOSOMES IN A [BOY]

1 2 3 4 5 6 7 8

9 10 11 12 13 14 15

16 17 18 19 20 21 22 X Y

THESE PROPELLER-LIKE THINGS ARE HOW WE DRAW CHROMOSOMES. THEY SORT OF LOOK A BIT LIKE THIS WHEN YOU LOOK AT THEM UNDER A MICROSCOPE. THERE ARE 23 PAIRS, THE REGULAR CHROMOSOMES NUMBERED 1—22 AND THE SPECIAL SEX CHROMOSOMES (X) AND (Y). THE CHROMOSOMES 1-22 ARE NUMBERED IN SIZE ORDER FROM THE LARGEST TO THE SMALLEST — WELL, NOT QUITE, BECAUSE (21) AND (22) ARE THE WRONG WAY ROUND. I GUESS SOMEONE MADE A MISTAKE WHEN THEY WERE ORIGINALLY DOING THE NUMBERS, AS CHROMOSOME (21) IS THE SMALLEST. YOU CAN SEE FROM THE (X) AND THE (Y) CHROMOSOME THAT THESE ARE THE CHROMOSOMES FROM A BOY.
AND YES, THE (Y) CHROMOSOME IS A LOT SMALLER THAN THE (X) CHROMOSOME.
(SORRY, BOYS)

maybe that's what it will become like, all this talk of designer babies. Just as I was musing these ideas over, Mum cleared her throat and began again.

Mum's Jottings 2b: A Girl's Chromosomes

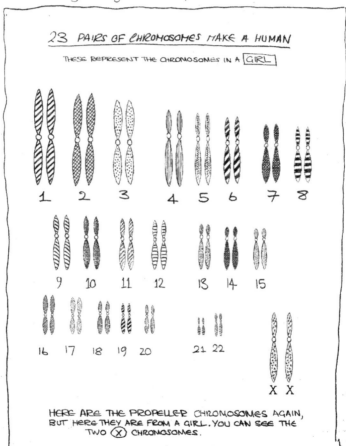

Half from your mum and half from your dad

Mum started by saying that we each had a mum and a dad. Now it didn't take a genius, or a scientist even, to work that one out. Everyone knew that. Then she explained that we were a little bit of both of them in the way we might look, and other characteristics. Fortunately I had the best bits of both my parents, perhaps even exceeding them in some aspects, and my brother Charlie was definitely the worst bits multiplied by ten. In fact, maybe he qualifies as a new sub-species. The reason that we are a bit of both became evident. We got one half of our chromosome pairs from our mum, and one half from our dad. Mum furtively began drawing as she explained that a baby was made by two types of sex cells (gametes) coming together. One was an egg from the mother. And the second sex cell was a sperm from the father. These sex cells are special because, unlike all our normal body cells, they only have half a set of the chromosome pairs in them. The reason for this becomes obvious: when you put two of these cells together, fuse them (as in making babies), they then have a complete set of chromosome pairs, one half from the mother and one half from the father. That way you get a new individual. That really was neat, and even I could follow Mum's erratic drawing style (Mum's Jottings 3).

So if I was right then, I was made up of a total of 46 chromosomes, arranged into 23 pairs. One set of the 23 pairs was from Mum, and one set was from Dad, and because I was a boy I had an XY pair. I was fine with that, but then couldn't work out why my brother Charlie, while having some family resemblance, was also quite different. Why did he have different coloured hair and eyes, and why were his ears a different shape? Surely he would have 23 chromosomes from Mum and 23 chromosomes from Dad. So why wasn't he exactly the same? Mum then explained that while we both got 23 chromosomes from each of them they wouldn't necessarily be exactly the same 23. Mum could see that I was looking confused. She rummaged around in the cupboard and came back with two boxes of straws. A speckled set and a striped set.

Mum's Jottings 3: How to Make a Human

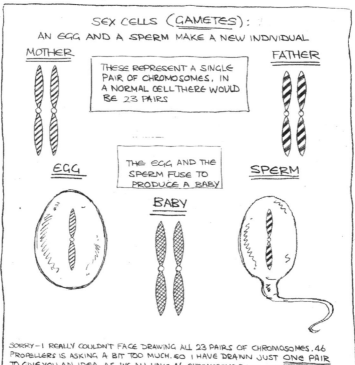

SEX CELLS (GAMETES):

AN EGG AND A SPERM MAKE A NEW INDIVIDUAL

MOTHER

FATHER

THESE REPRESENT A SINGLE PAIR OF CHROMOSOMES, IN A NORMAL CELL THERE WOULD BE 23 PAIRS

EGG

THE EGG AND THE SPERM FUSE TO PRODUCE A BABY

SPERM

BABY

SORRY – I REALLY COULDN'T FACE DRAWING ALL 23 PAIRS OF CHROMOSOMES. 46 PROPELLERS IS ASKING A BIT TOO MUCH. SO I HAVE DRAWN JUST ONE PAIR TO GIVE YOU AN IDEA. AS WE ALL HAVE 46 CHROMOSOMES YOU CAN SEE TO MAKE A BABY IT WOULD BE DISASTROUS TO JUST FUSE 2 CELLS HAVING 46 CHROMOSOMES EACH AS YOU WOULD END UP WITH 92 CHROMOSOMES! ONE SET TOO MANY. TO GET ROUND THIS WE HAVE TO HALVE OUR CHROMOSOME NUMBER WHEN WE ARE MAKING OUR EGG OR OUR SPERM (SEX CELLS) SO THAT WHEN THEY FUSE TOGETHER, THEY HAVE THE RIGHT TOTAL OF 46 CHROMOSOMES. BASICALLY, THE 23 PAIRS OF CHROMOSOMES SEPARATE, SO JUST ONE HALF GO INTO THE SEX CELLS. THEN WHEN THEY FUSE, THE RIGHT CHROMOSOMES PAIR UP AGAIN TO MAKE A FULL SET.

"Imagine," she said, "that the speckled set are my chromosomes and the striped set are Dad's." She then arranged them carefully into 23 pairs, writing 1-22 and X and Y on them. "Now, here is the complicated bit." She wasn't kidding! "You need to remember that my chromosomes come from Grandma and Grandad Ward, and Dad's come from Grandma and Grandad Davison, so the chromosomes making up each pair are different." Mum now put a spot on one of each pair of her chromosome straws, and a spot on each one of Dad's. "Let's say that the ones with the spots on come from the Grandmas and the ones without are the chromosomes from the Grandads." Then she explained that when the sex cells were being formed, the egg could have any mixture of spotted and unspotted chromosomes, and so could the sperm. That way Charlie and I could have different chromosomes coming originally from different grandparents. That was cool. That explained why Charlie had the same hair as Grandma Davison, and I had the same eyes as Grandma Ward and Mum. Of course you could keep going back and tracing the chromosomes from our grandparents' parents and so on. We could trace our genetic inheritance right back to our original ancestors if we had enough information.

However – there is always a however – it isn't quite that simple. The chromosomes wouldn't be exactly the same. Mum explained that the "spotted" and "unspotted" chromosomes could actually swap bits, and so that would change them to some extent from the original grandparental chromosomes, and of course that process has been happening each time chromosomes are passed on. That explained why we are all individuals. Still, we thought that was enough detail for now. Check out Mum's straws in Mum's Jottings 4.

"Look, how about I finish with trying to explain where James got his ears from?" said Mum. The others perked up a bit at this, as I displayed my famous Davison ears, a feature easily recognised in the male Davison line. Charlie was not blessed with this feature and had Mum's ears; clearly they had less distinctive ears in the Ward family. Mum disappeared and came back with a photograph

Mum's Jottings 4: Inheritance

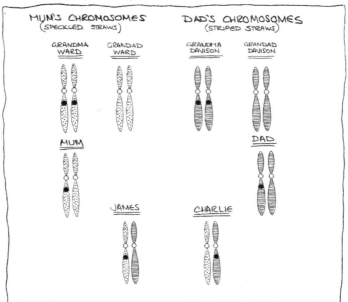

MUM'S CHROMOSOMES (SPECKLED STRAWS)   DAD'S CHROMOSOMES (STRIPED STRAWS)

GRANDMA WARD   GRANDAD WARD   GRANDMA DAVISON   GRANDAD DAVISON

MUM   DAD

JAMES   CHARLIE

THE SPECKLED AND STRIPED STRAWS ARE DRAWN AS CHROMOSOME PROPELLERS THE SAME AS IN THE OTHER DIAGRAMS. BECAUSE IT IS TOO DIFFICULT TO LOOK AT ALL 23 PAIRS OF CHROMOSOMES WE WILL JUST LOOK AT ONE PAIR.

THE CHROMOSOMES WITH SPOTS ON ARE THE ONES THAT ORIGINALLY CAME FROM THE GRANDMAS. IF WE THINK OF JAMES' BROWN EYES, THEY COULD HAVE COME FROM GRANDMA WARD, AND CHARLIE'S HAIR COLOUR COULD HAVE COME FROM GRANDMA DAVISON. OBVIOUSLY, THIS IS VERY SIMPLIFIED AND IS JUST SHOWING ONE PAIR OF CHROMOSOMES AND ONE POSSIBLE OPTION.

Mum's Jottings 4: Inheritance...Continued

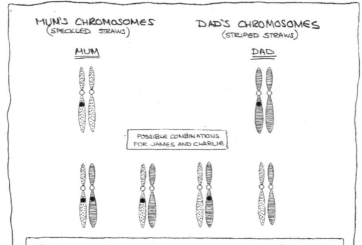

MUM'S CHROMOSOMES
(SPECKLED STRAWS)

DAD'S CHROMOSOMES
(STRIPED STRAWS)

MUM

DAD

POSSIBLE COMBINATIONS
FOR JAMES AND CHARLIE

THIS IS STILL SHOWING YOU JUST ONE PAIR OF CHROMOSOMES, BUT I HAVE DRAWN ALL THE POSSIBLE OPTIONS THAT YOU COULD GET FROM MUM AND DAD. YOU CAN SEE ALL THE COMBINATIONS OF CHROMOSOMES THAT YOU CAN HAVE COMING DOWN FROM GRANDPARENTS

THIS IS JUST A SIMPLIFICATION, AND OF COURSE IT IS ACTUALLY MORE COMPLICATED THAN THIS. I DON'T WANT TO WORRY YOU WITH TOO MUCH DETAIL, BUT HERE GOES. WHEN THE SEX CELLS (EGGS IN WOMEN AND SPERM IN MEN) ARE FORMED, BEFORE THE PAIRS OF CHROMOSOMES GO THEIR OWN WAY INTO SEPARATE EGGS AND SPERM, THEY CAN ACTUALLY SWAP BITS OF DNA. SO EFFECTIVELY, SOME OF THE GRANDPARENTAL CHROMOSOMES GET MIXED.

CONSIDER MY CHROMOSOMES FROM MY PARENTS, GRANDMA WARD AND GRANDAD WARD (THE SPECKLED ONES). WHEN THE EGG THAT PRODUCED JAMES WAS BEING MADE, MY SPOTTED CHROMOSOME WOULD HAVE SWOPPED BITS WITH MY UNSPOTTED CHROMOSOME. THIS MEANS THAT THE SPECKLED CHROMOSOME PASSED ON TO JAMES WOULD BE A MIXTURE OF HIS GRANDPARENTS' CHROMOSOMES, ALTHOUGH THERE MIGHT HAVE BEEN JUST A TINY BIT OF SWAPPING AND SO IT MIGHT APPEAR TO COME FROM JUST ONE GRANDPARENT. OF COURSE THE SAME PROCESS IS GOING ON WITH HIS DAD'S CHROMOSOMES FORMING THE SPERM. ALL THIS ADDS TO HOW DIFFERENT WE ALL ARE AND MEANS THAT EACH PERSON IS UNIQUE.

of myself, Dad, Grandad Davison and Great-Grandad Davison. There we were all lined up for a family photo, and our ears were well displayed.

"Right, now let's see if we can trace the Davison family 'ear gene'," said Mum.

"That's easy," I said.

"Go on then." Mum handed me the pens.

Everyone fell about laughing at my effort to draw the family photograph showing the Davison ears. However, they all stopped laughing when I was able to show the inheritance of the Davison ear gene (James' Jottings 3).

We decided that it had been a very long session, and that we should call it a day. There was only so much genetics a boy could take, even in the endeavour to clone a genius, and what we all needed to do right now was to run around the garden with a football like lunatics. As Katie quite rightly observed, given that boys seemed to have a monopoly on this primitive behaviour, it was scientific evidence that the primitive instinct gene was most probably on the Y chromosome.

James' Jottings 3: Inheritance of the Gene for Davison Ears

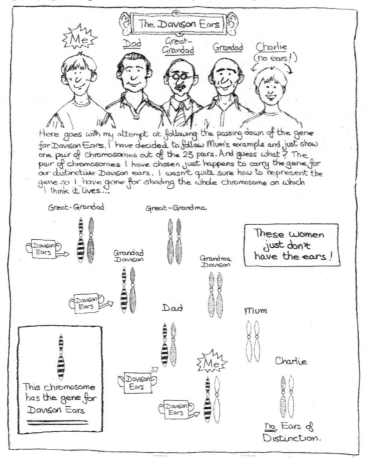

Here goes with my attempt at following the passing down of the gene for Davison Ears. I have decided to follow Mum's example and just show one pair of chromosomes out of the 23 pairs. And guess what? The pair of chromosomes I have chosen just happens to carry the gene for our distinctive Davison ears. I wasn't quite sure how to represent the gene so I have gone for shading the whole chromosome on which I think it lives....

RIVALS

At the start of the holidays it had seemed like we had ages, but now there was little time left and the competition deadline loomed. We were all anxious that the holidays would soon come to an end and our project would still be unfinished. We certainly had learnt a lot, but didn't feel we were close to producing our own first super-human clone. On top of all that the competition seemed to be hotting up. I didn't mean from the nerdy crew either, although their domestic house-robot project was apparently looking very good. No, it seemed that everyone else in the world was trying to clone a human. Maybe I was just being paranoid, but every time I glanced at a newspaper there seemed to be something on cloning. Big, bold print headlines seemed to be taunting me.

"Italian Doctor Says He Will Clone Humans."

"Scientists Say It Is Feasible To Clone."

"Designer Babies…Clone To Order."

There was even some claim that they would bring the woolly mammoth back. That was exciting, but this was getting serious. It must be a good idea because everyone was trying to do it. It wasn't fair, but as Mum always said, nothing is fair and especially in the case of love, war and the advancement of science.

We called an emergency meeting round at my house to discuss tactics.

"Maybe we should go for something smaller. Does anyone have any pets?" I asked.

I had a small pet in mind, sort of hamster-sized. That was it, didn't Luke's sister have a hamster?

"Hey, Luke, what about Alex's hamster? Could we sort of borrow that?" I said hopefully. Luke looked unhappy.

"I thought we agreed, no animal experimentation, strictly human," said Luke.

"What about Charlie, he's the smallest human we know," said Ed.

"I don't think Mum would be too impressed if we practised on him. What if it all went horribly wrong, and we succeeded in getting two Charlies? Mum would go berserk," I laughed. "Besides, from what I remember it's the size of the total DNA and not the size of the individual that is important. I've got a horrible feeling that there isn't much difference between ourselves and other animals. But still, I think we should get hold of a small animal, easier to handle, so that we are ready to have a trial run." I looked round for support.

"There is one very big problem," said Katie.

"What's that?" we chorused.

"Apart from knowing a little about the basics of genetics, we still have no idea how to clone, or even where to begin," said Katie glumly.

She was absolutely right, we didn't have the first clue. There was no way that we could proceed without further instructions. There was nothing for it, we had to go back to Mum for more lessons. We decided to brace ourselves. Almost three packets of Jaffa cakes later and we were ready to go. The competition might be ahead at the moment but they didn't know what they were up against.

7

LESSON THREE – CLONING AT LAST

M um was more than a little surprised when we came hunting her down for more genetics lessons. She conceded that time was getting on, and the deadline getting closer. We managed to convince her that we were going to do a schools information leaflet on genetics and enter the "Explaining Science" category of the competition, whatever that was, rather than the more glamorous "New Inventions" category. How embarrassing to be such intellectual geeks! Still, it was all in a good cause.

We had a quick recap of what we had already learnt and remembered. I was impressed. We could struggle through the basics of DNA being a code, a sort of instruction manual for making an individual, and we could even follow inheritance, the passing of a particular characteristic through a family. Now we explained that we really wanted to know about cloning.

What is cloning?

Mum said that in genetics there were two meanings of the word cloning, just to be confusing.

"The first is used when someone has discovered a gene and has managed to cut it out of the genome, or separate the DNA that made up the gene. The papers would then say the gene for blah has been cloned."

"Wait a minute, what's this genome thing?" I asked.

Mum realised she had lapsed into jargon again. She backtracked and explained that the whole sequence of DNA that was used to make an individual was called a genome. So all the DNA in the 46 chromosomes together made a human genome. She then explained that this was the reason for the name of the big project that had been in the news, The Human Genome Project, where scientists from all over the world were working out the entire sequence of DNA that made a human. In fact, the genome had now been sequenced.

"Does that mean we already have the instructions for making a human?" asked Ed.

"Well, we have a lot of the basic information, but just knowing the DNA sequence in a human doesn't mean we know how it all works. For example, you could go outside and dismantle my car. You would have all the bits, but unless you know how they all work together you won't be able to make a car that works," said Mum. She thought for a bit and then started again. "But we can get round that, and potentially make a human by cloning, the second meaning of cloning."

This was what we wanted to hear.

The second meaning of cloning, the type of cloning we were interested in, was the cloning of an organism. Mum explained that this was when an identical genetic copy was made. So if we had Alex's hamster and cloned it, we would have an identical hamster with exactly the same DNA.

Identical twins

Mum then told us that identical twins were actually nature's way of cloning. They really were genetically identical. So humans had already been cloned.

We all racked our brains trying to think of any identical twins that we knew. We could only think of twins that were not identical. That was it, we wanted to know what the difference was between identical and non-identical twins.

"That's easy," said Luke.

We all waited for an enlightening, earth-shattering piece of information.

"Whether they have the same or different DNA," he finished.

"UHHH."

"Well, he is absolutely right, but I imagine that you all want to know how that comes about," said Mum.

She told us to remember back to when we had learnt about what made an individual: that you needed an egg and a sperm each containing 23 chromosomes to come together and make a new individual containing the right number of 46 chromosomes. So far, so good. However, she said that when they fused together to make a baby, you didn't actually get a baby straight away. That made sense, otherwise why would it take so long being pregnant? In fact, to start with there was just a clump of cells and these divided and changed over time to make a baby. Well, in the case of identical twins, very early on this clump of cells go a bit awry on their dividing, and actually manage to split into two clumps instead of staying together as one. So when this happens, you have a bonus baby, you get identical twins made from the same starting DNA. To complete the story, twins that are not identical are genetically the same as normal brothers and sisters, they just happen to be born at the same time. Weird. Imagine sharing Mum's womb with Charlie! Sibling rivalry could really start early. Basically, it was just sheer chance that two eggs and two sperm containing the parents' DNA decide to get together, or fuse, at the same time.

So in a nutshell, or should I say womb: you get identical twins with the same genetic material, from the fusion of one egg and one sperm; and non-identical twins from two different eggs and two different sperm each fusing separately at the same time.

Looking around at the others I could tell that we were all thinking the same thing. Given that old Mother Nature could manage to clone, and had been doing so for years, how come someone hadn't already cloned a human? Mum also could sense this looming question. She explained that until the end of the last century we weren't very good at making "test tube" babies. These were babies that were started outside of the mother, by fusing together an egg and a sperm (not quite in a test tube, but that's where the name comes from), and then once the cells had started to divide they were put safely back inside the mother as an embryo, a very early stage of a baby. I thought it was all getting a bit tedious and wished she would give the background detail a miss and move straight to actual cloning. My attention returned as she explained that the technology of extracting certain cells and keeping them alive used not to be very good but had now improved, making cloning feasible.

"So," she concluded, "scientists have made a lot of progress in recent years and it is now possible, in theory, to clone a human."

Dolly the sheep

Mum thought that perhaps she should explain about cloning by using an example. She guessed that we might have heard about Dolly, a very famous sheep which was the first animal to be cloned. We pricked up our ears at this moment. Alex's hamster perhaps could join this hall of fame. Mum mentioned that in the Science museum there was a jumper made from the wool that had come from Dolly. What a way to go: you would think that there would be more to celebrity than having a jumper in the museum. What could you make from a hamster, I wondered.

Mum continued. "To put it simply, Dolly was made by taking a cell from one sheep and putting it into an empty egg cell of another sheep. So, if we consider humans, instead of having 23 chromosomes coming from the mother's egg and 23 chromosomes coming from the father's sperm to make a baby, you have the whole 46 chromosomes from a cell of one individual. Hence a genetic clone."

Mum paused for breath and looked up. She was met by blank, staring faces.

"Okay, perhaps that was a little too fast. I'll try again."

Out came the paper and pencils and she was off, a little more slowly this time.

She reminded us that all of our cells contain an entire copy of our DNA, our genome, and that is what makes us an individual. If we could somehow take that DNA and make another person, then they would be genetically identical to us, our clone. So how would it work to clone an animal of our choice?

Scrawling frantically on the piece of paper, Mum began to explain.

"To make Dolly, first the scientists had to catch the sheep they wanted to clone, and then obtain a cell containing the DNA. I have no idea what this sheep was called, let's say she was called Molly. Molly's DNA was then used to make the clone, Dolly. So Dolly has the same DNA as her...an identical twin if you like, separated by time. Molly was a six-year-old ewe and the cell was taken from a mammary gland, a boob cell to you, or udder if you prefer. Okay, so that cell contains all the DNA you need, but it is not in the right state, the right form, to be accepted as the DNA to start a new baby lamb." Mum paused to check we were hanging in there. Barely.

"Let me explain that a little bit. As we said at the start, all cells in a human contain the same genome, the same DNA, the same genes. But not all cells in the body are the same, there are different types that do different functions. A bone cell will behave differently to a heart cell but they all have the same genome, the same DNA. So how might the control centre of each cell make that DNA behave differently?" Mum looked up hoping for some answers. We stared blankly.

"Could you not alter the DNA in some way?" I asked tentatively.

"Yes, you could. Remember that there are many genes doing many things."

"Could you cut out some of the genes? That would stop them working," said Katie.

"Or block them like a road block," said Ed.

"Yes, that's exactly what the different cells do. In their control centres, the nucleus, the genome is tailored to their needs. Only the genes that are needed to work in that type of cell are switched on and the genes that are not needed are switched off.

"So, the DNA can give instructions for a heart cell to behave differently from a bone cell. This is a bit like taking a book and changing the pages you read to get a different story, but all the time you have the full copy of the book. This means that the DNA in different cells is programmed DNA, it can only make that type of cell. If you want DNA to be able to make any and every cell, brain cells, bone cells, heart cells and many more, then you have to use DNA that hasn't already been programmed. New, fresh DNA, just like the DNA in the cells of an embryo, a new baby. It is the un-programmed DNA that is needed for cloning."

"But I thought you said that they took an udder cell, that would only have udder DNA," I asked.

"Maybe they were going to clone a huge udder, invasion of the giant udders," laughed Luke.

"You're right, to a point. This was the hard bit for the scientists, getting the DNA in the mammary gland, the udder cell, to be like the DNA in the first few cells that make a baby lamb, and not for it to think it was udder-cell DNA. So they used lots of chemicals and things like electric shocks to de-programme the DNA. That way it could become anything, including all the cells needed to make a new individual. Once the DNA in the cell from Molly was behaving like new DNA, it could then be used to make a baby lamb."

"How can it be used to make a new baby lamb?" asked Katie.

"Well, remember, normally to make a new human individual you have the mother's egg with half the chromosomes and the father's sperm with half the chromosomes, and they fuse to make an individual with the usual full number of chromosomes. For cloning you need an egg from a female, but you need to empty out her DNA, then you can put in your de-programmed DNA which has the full number of chromosomes already. So in this case a sheep was chosen, and an egg taken and emptied. This sheep not only donates the egg that will be emptied, but is also used to carry the baby, the pregnancy. The sheep in this case is technically known as a surrogate mother, meaning that she will have the baby but that she is not biologically the mother. Basically you use the surrogate mother's empty egg, and then you implant the 'fertilised' egg in her womb. Molly's DNA, taken from one of her udder cells, was de-programmed and then put inside the donated empty egg, and the egg thought it had been fertilised and started to divide. At this point the egg was then put back into the surrogate mother sheep. A normal pregnancy followed and Dolly was born, who was genetically identical to Molly, and was the first animal clone." Mum sighed, not quite with relief, but she had finished.

This was heavy going even with the diagrams. You can see Mum's attempts in Mum's Jottings 5. I, along with the others, was beginning to have doubts as to whether we stood a chance of cloning anything. I was impressed that I had got this far with my understanding, but wasn't sure I

Mum's Jottings 5: Cloning

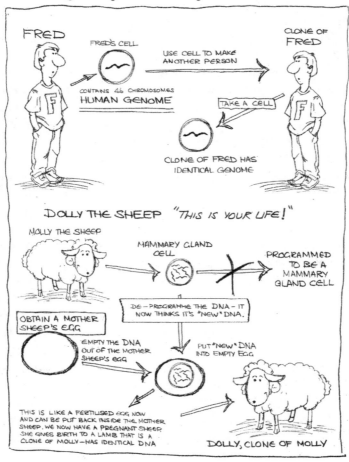

FRED

CLONE OF FRED

FRED'S CELL

USE CELL TO MAKE ANOTHER PERSON

CONTAINS 46 CHROMOSOMES
HUMAN GENOME

TAKE A CELL

CLONE OF FRED HAS IDENTICAL GENOME

DOLLY THE SHEEP "THIS IS YOUR LIFE!"

MOLLY THE SHEEP

MAMMARY GLAND CELL

PROGRAMMED TO BE A MAMMARY GLAND CELL

DE-PROGRAMME THE DNA - IT NOW THINKS IT'S "NEW" DNA.

OBTAIN A MOTHER SHEEP'S EGG

EMPTY THE DNA OUT OF THE MOTHER SHEEP'S EGG

PUT "NEW" DNA INTO EMPTY EGG

THIS IS LIKE A FERTILISED EGG NOW AND CAN BE PUT BACK INSIDE THE MOTHER SHEEP. WE NOW HAVE A PREGNANT SHEEP. SHE GIVES BIRTH TO A LAMB THAT IS A CLONE OF MOLLY—HAS IDENTICAL DNA

DOLLY, CLONE OF MOLLY

could get much further. I grappled with the old brain for a few minutes, and then tentatively tried to talk myself through what I had just heard. Taking it from the top, and making the assumption that it was Alex's hamster that was to be cloned, first I needed a cell from Alex's hamster. Then I had to make the DNA in that cell think it was as new, that it had no misplaced ideas of what it was, completely fool it into thinking it hadn't been used at all; a sort of debriefing. Then I had to find another poor, unsuspecting hamster of the female variety, nick one of its eggs (I won't bore you with the gory dissection skills needed here) and then empty out the DNA already in the egg. All that was needed then was to put the two things together, the new DNA and the egg, and hey presto, you had the beginnings of a baby hamster. Well, you did have to stick this egg back into the surrogate hamster somehow so that it had a normal pregnancy. Even the thought of that was too much for me. How did you go about sticking anything back in a hamster? I was beginning to feel queasy now and my enthusiasm for a practical demonstration of cloning was fading. I realised that I didn't even know how many chromosomes a hamster had. I think that Alex's hamster was home and dry, it would never know just how close it was to becoming famous. Just as well really. Check out Alex's hamster in James' Jottings 4.

James' Jottings 4: Hamster Clone

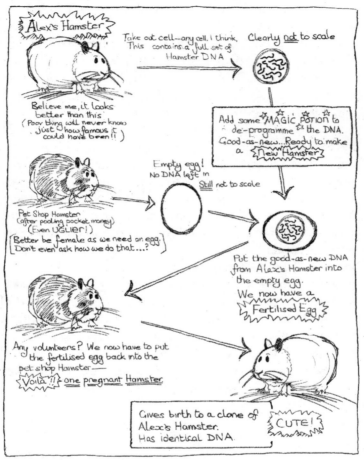

CLONE WARS

We were all feeling somewhat deflated, and even a little foolish, to think we had seriously thought we might try cloning. One consolation, we had a much better knowledge of genetics now, light years ahead of where we were at the beginning of the holiday. Okay, I know that's not difficult considering our starting point. Strangely though, it had been interesting, and I almost missed our lessons. Almost.

Mum was a little perplexed when we said that we weren't entering the "Explaining Science" competition after all. We told her that we really would have liked to come up with a "new invention", but now knew that genetics was out of the question. She conceded that it would have been very ambitious.

"After all, what were you thinking of doing, cloning a human?" were her very words. Just how right she was she will never know.

We pooled together some of our pocket money and bought her a box of chocolates, which seemed to do the trick. She said it had been a pleasure to teach us, and that she would be happy to help anytime.

Just when we thought we had escaped, Mum called us back and said that even though we weren't entering the competition, she had some questions for us. She wanted us to think about whether we should clone animals and humans. Would we have clones in the future? Would this be a good or a bad thing?

PART 2

CLONE WARS: OUR STORY

1

A WORLD OF HAVES
AND HAVE-NOTS

It is the middle of the 22nd century and life on the whole is good for most people. Technology has advanced far beyond our ancestors' dreams and there is barely anything now that is worth lifting a finger for, apart from the nation's latest game craze, Clone Wars.

I should first introduce myself and my friends. My name is James, and my friends are Ed, Luke and Katie. We are very fortunate to be part of the genetically élite, not a single rogue gene in any one of us. We were bred to perfection, using tried and tested combinations of genes. We are all of us different, life would be so boring if we were all identical…like the clones, but I will come back to that. We are lucky enough to come from good gene pools; which means our ancestors had no horrendous gene mutations. I should perhaps give you some historical background. Let's go back to the Gene Proclamation Bill, which was introduced in the middle of the 21st century. It stated that all families who wished to continue their genetic line and have their own children, had to prove that their ancestral genes were good. This involved tracing all family members and subjecting them to a genetic profiling test: that is, getting a complete sequence of their genome and comparing it with all the known genetic mutations that cause disease or disability. Only those who could prove that they were not carriers of genetic disease, and had no physical or intellectual impairments, were allowed to have children using their own genes. Each individual had to have a validated breeding certificate before they could have their own children. That certificate stated whether you were allowed to use your own genes or not, and how many children you were allowed to have. Not surprisingly, the better your genes, the more children you were allowed. Borderline cases were only allowed one, and most people were allowed two. I am always in awe of those families who have four children: imagine what their genes are like!

Now, even if you are allowed to have your own genetic children, nothing can be left to chance. There is none of that random mixing of 23 chromosomes from your mother and 23 chromosomes from your father, which sounds gross. No, the embryos are all produced and checked at the Genetic Control Centre, and in many cases the genes are modified, or tweaked, to make each child that bit better than the parents. I do think some of the parents go over the top in adjusting their kids. I mean, take the family down the road – the kids are well over average height, and have unnaturally blond hair. It's difficult to spot any family resemblance, especially when the parents are bordering on the short side of acceptable and have sort of yucky dung-coloured hair. Still, as Dad says, there are always those who want to be flashy. Me and my friends, we're relatively normal and there's definitely nothing flashy about us. I guess that's why we stick together.

That brings me on to the clones, and those poor unfortunates who aren't able to use their own genes to have children. If your breeding certificate is stamped inferior then you are only allowed to breed clones. Even that is not easy. What I understand comes from overheard conversations, and Katie, who seems to find out everything. Basically, the clone breeders are graded using both intelligence and physical fitness tests. Then, depending on their score, they are assigned an appropriate level of clone. You wouldn't want to do those tests on a bad day. The genetic clones are produced from a range of graded DNA. The types are: Superior – the intellectual clones; Standard-Physical – the sports and battle clones; Standard-Intellect – the top worker clones, and Basic – the normal worker clones. There are a variety of clones within each class so that they don't all look exactly the same, but it is still relatively easy to spot them. Ironically, many of them look a little too perfect, too symmetrical compared to the mixed genes of the genetically élite. Because of this, many breeding with their own genes often choose to keep a quirky feature to ensure family resemblance, and to avoid the embarrassment of being mistaken for a clone. Take me for example. I have family ears that you wouldn't call genetically perfect.

I imagine if I had been born without all these checks, back in the time of my great-great-grandfather, I would have taken my chances, made do with the genes dealt me. It would have been normal then. It is difficult now, though, to think of a world without all of these controls ensuring that we are the best products genes can provide. To some we seem a very privileged society, and the authorities are constantly reminding us of this. Genetics and Society, basically the importance of keeping the gene pool pure, come high on our school curriculum. However, despite all these controls there are still some babies born with mutations, throwbacks to when everyone was allowed to breed. Rumours circulating in school say that these poor creatures accidentally born today are kept hidden away on remote islands, and used for experimental purposes. It conjures up images of a zombie island, and I guess these are the bogeymen of our times.

THE GAME

I mentioned there is only one thing worth lifting a finger for, and that is playing a virtual reality computer game called Clone Wars. This came in a few years back and quickly became a national craze. It is a futuristic battle of gladiators with technology strapped on. It is awesome.

Computer games have gone way beyond the science fiction of the past. And the virtual reality world of games – cyber world – goes beyond imagination. It is difficult to know where the real and the virtual boundaries are. Many people can hook into the cyber world at home, but there are also cyber cafés and cyber parks everywhere. You can just walk in, swipe your ID card, and you have instant access. While parents are generally happy for their kids to access their virtual classroom, they are equally unhappy about how much time they spend hooking up to games in cyber world. This has become such a worry that the authorities have limited the access of minors, that is, all of us under-eighteens, by putting restrictions on our ID cards. Even so, there are still fears of the increasing number of cyber junkies, those who have difficulty distinguishing between real and virtual. These pale, lifeless souls are seen walking the streets from cyber café to cyber park. The worker clones are thought to be especially susceptible to this affliction, and so are banned from entering cyber world.

It sounds pretty bleak, but for the majority of people this is not the case. Life is good, and the games are a great way to enjoy your spare time: real escapism. So what is this Clone Wars that has the country enthralled? As the title suggests, this is a battle between clones, not real ones, of course, but virtual clones, and the one left alive is the winner. Well, it's a bit more sophisticated than that, but that's the gist of it.

To start with, you select your basic clone from the cyber world gene pool, and before entering the qualifying round you are allowed to modify up to three genes. In the qualifying round you have to win three battles out of five, and for each battle you win you can then modify another gene. So for every clone that qualifies you have a basic clone with a minimum of six, and a maximum of eight, gene modifications. Then before entry into the competitive knock-out rounds, a further two gene modifications are allowed, making a total of eight to ten modifications. The rest of the competition is based on straight knock-out rules. Clones are drawn at random to battle, and if you win you go through to the next round and if not you're out. Those reaching the quarter-finals are allowed a further two gene modifications, and the same at the semi-finals. The finalists can make just one last gene modification before the final. By now these clones are barely recognisable from the humble basic clone that started, having between thirteen and fifteen major gene modifications each. Oh, the other thing I should mention is that the game is played in a series of arenas, from wasteland, through city, jungle, and on to outer space. Initially you select the arena you want to compete in, and clearly you make gene modifications to suit your environment. However, there is a supreme championship in which all the winners of each arena compete. This takes place in an arena generated randomly by the computer. So some competitors, with the supreme cup in mind, may decide to carry out gene modifications that might be advantageous in many different environments rather than ones that are just specific to their chosen battle arena. It's a fine balance of adaptation. In fact, it is like playing at Nature, a modern Darwinian game of survival of the fittest. To make the game more interesting, in each arena there are a series of hidden weapons or tools that may be useful in battle, and on top of that the computer generates its own rogue clones, two random clones which may join in the battle. The game is a real test of skill, strategy and nerve.

As a competitor you take on the role of the clone you have generated; not for the faint-hearted. But you can also enter as a spectator. People pay lots of money for these ringside seats, although they are not your usual seats. You are there as part of the scenery, and you can imagine how intense it gets. Everyone says that it is pretty scary just being in the arena as a spectator. One poor guy was once mauled by one of the computer's rogue clones because his spectator ID wasn't showing, and he was mistaken for a competitor. I know that this is only virtual, so he didn't suffer any physical damage, but he was a gibbering wreck. This is a game for control freaks and adrenalin junkies. I guess life has become too comfortable and easy for people these days, so there is a need for some raw excitement.

Like all competitive sports, if you can call it a sport, there are favourites that are rooted for, and then there are those competitors everyone loves to hate. The current bad guy goes by the name of Claws, and has the most amazing razor-like talons on his hands. These are used to rip other clones to shreds, leaving more than one with a face hanging with ribbons of flesh. Our hero of the moment is Iron Jaw: he looks like one of the muscle-bound comic-book heroes of the past, a real retro look, quite funny really. But he is incredibly strong, and clearly has had some gene modifications to help him outsmart the other clones. It is thought that these two will be the finalists this year, and it is expected to be one hell of a battle.

SCHOOLS COMPETITION

It was amazing when we had our very own chance to enter that kind of battle. I can still remember the day when it all started.

Ambling into school one morning, I could sense an air of excitement. Something good must be going down.

"Hey, James, have you heard?" shouted Ed.

"Clearly not! What's all the fuss about?" I asked.

"The makers of Clone Wars have announced a schools competition based on the original Clone Wars, but this one is to be Animal Clone Wars," finished Ed, barely pausing for breath.

During a rare full-school assembly – we usually had assemblies on our classroom terminal links – the headmaster made the formal announcement that we had all been waiting for. His face loomed down on us from the huge screens in the stadium-sized hall. There was an undercurrent of murmuring and an almost electric crackling in the air, not this time caused by the collective gathering of manmade jumpers!

"Students, I would like to draw your attention to the announcement of a schools competition entitled 'Animal Clones – The Battle of the Beasts.' A little graphic for my liking, but no doubt appealing to yourselves. Each school will be permitted to enter one animal clone. I have decided…"

This was it, the old windbag was going to say that only those with a genetically engineered IQ above infinity could take part. But I was wrong.

"…that we should have our own school competition, not a battle you understand, but all of you wishing to participate may generate your own clone. Our cyber world access park has been linked into the appropriate programmes so you will be able to use those facilities. For those of you wishing to work from home, the school has been issued with an access number which can be obtained from the school office. This can only be used in conjunction with your personal pupil ID. There will be one month for you to generate your prototype clone. Then, in true democratic style, you may all vote for your choice. I will make the final announcement of the successful clone five weeks from today."

The screen reverted to the school crest, the assembly was over.

The day wasn't quite a write-off, but nobody could think or talk of anything other than the competition, and what wicked ideas they had for a clone. There was also a certain amount of secretiveness. As usual, everyone was under the delusion that their idea was so fantastic and cool that the whole world and his dog wanted to copy it. Ed and I decided that we would work together, perhaps with Katie and Luke. We would see them at lunch time when the specialist subsections of the school came together.

We met Katie and Luke straight after lunch down by the benches on the far boundary of the school's campus. We sat on our usual bench and discussed the competition. One thing was for certain, we were going to take part and we desperately wanted to win. Apart from that, there was little else on which we could agree.

"What are the basic clones that are available?" asked Katie.

Luke shrugged. "No one has accessed the programme details yet, but the rumour is that only four major classes of the animal kingdom are included: mammals, birds, reptiles and insects."

"So I guess they will concentrate on land arenas, given that there are no fish or amphibians. Still, that leaves lots of possible choices, even just with mammals." I was already wondering about a choice of clone.

"We could check out the major predators?" suggested Ed.

"It's usually best to have something that has all-round ability without any obvious weaknesses. Good defence, attack and intelligence," Luke said.

"A big cat…"

"An alligator…"

"A giant rattlesnake…no, a…"

Everyone was talking at once.

"Look, we need to give this some serious thought, go away and do some research, brush up on our biology, adaptation and survival stuff, then we can make a choice," I suggested.

Everyone agreed.

"We really need to take a proper look at the programme before we can make any choices, let alone designing and modifying our clone. I think it's available tomorrow," said Katie.

She was right of course. We agreed not to talk about it further until we had all the options and some basic facts to work with, some real data.

ANIMAL CLONE

A week later we met up round at my house, all armed with our "Tipdats", small handheld computer databases (data at your fingertips, or so the advertising slogan goes), bursting at the seams with downloaded information. Having demolished sufficient snacks to keep our brains from glucose starvation (though I suspect the amount of blood that was being diverted to our stomachs to deal with the snack overload probably counteracted that theory), we were ready to discuss plans. Katie had come with a "need to know" outline of the game rules. She knew that we only operated on a minimum "need to know" basis. Too many facts were just plain confusing.

We crowded round Katie and read the rules over her shoulder. Although the game was based on the original Clone Wars it was simplified for the schools competition. This was to cope with the vast number of competitors expected – all schools were allowed to enter a clone, and as it was a National competition that was a large number of schools. All entry clones were allowed three gene modifications, the same as in Clone Wars. But thereafter the rules were slightly different. You had three qualifying rounds and had to win two of them. For each battle you won you were allowed to make two gene modifications. Once you made it through the qualifying rounds all the others were straight knock-out rounds, up to the final. If you won your battle you went through, and if you lost you were out. As simple as that.

To enter the competition, first of all we had to decide on our starting clone. I favoured a bird of prey, while Katie and Luke were keen to have a land mammal such as a big cat. Ed wasn't sure, and could see the merits of both. I could see that this could potentially run and run. We needed to make a decision so that we could concentrate on modifying our basic clone, making it deadly, literally.

"We could just toss a coin," I suggested.

So, relying completely on chance, that was it, one flip of a coin and we had selected a bird clone. Fortunately everyone was happy with the choice. We trawled our way through the different bird clones available, and unanimously agreed on an African crowned eagle. These eagles live and hunt in tropical forests and have talons so massive and sharp that they can stab right through the body of a monkey…pretty awesome. This clone was a great starting point to design the ultimate battle machine.

Having chosen our starting clone, we then had to decide which genes were to be modified. This was the tricky bit. Gene modification is fairly routine these days, and in theory there were no limitations. The help programme that came with the game instructions gave a few examples of genes that could be modified, and the possible advantages or even disadvantages that these could bring to your clone. We spent ages studying the examples. Clearly there were the obvious characteristics such as size, strength and potential weapons. There was a fearsome-looking tiger with the prehistoric tusks of the sabre-toothed tiger and a hawk with over-sized razor talons. Naturally, the programme had simplified some of the modifications, as we all know that many characteristics are the result of a number of genes acting together rather than just one single gene.

We thought long and hard about possible changes that we could make. These ranged from changing the talons and beak to such outrageous proportions that the clone could barely take off from the ground. However, we knew that in the early part of the competition there would be a vast array of clones with many different strengths and weaknesses. It was important that we didn't make our clone particularly vulnerable. A few conservative carefully chosen changes should make it a good all-rounder. Firstly, we decided to increase the strategic thinking of our eagle by increasing the size of one area of its brain. Secondly, we increased its wingspan to give it an edge on speed, and our final gene modification was to increase its visual acuity, which was already pretty good. But now it could detect small movements at a distance of several kilometres and, like the kestrel, could see ultraviolet light.

We agreed that we would take turns to enter cyber world as our clone. Whoever scored the highest on the practice arena would be the clone in the competition. All we had to do now was to register our clone, and officially name it. The naming caused almost as much disagreement as our original choice of clone. In the end the task was done, and Kingly was created. Our clone was born, a crowned king of the beasts — well, hopefully — in a virtual world.

MAIDEN FLIGHTS

We couldn't wait to take our maiden flights as Kingly in cyber world. I am sure it is the same of all proud parents, but we thought that Kingly was the most beautiful and splendid creature ever to exist and just like any new parent we had great hopes and aspirations. It was slightly weird, though, to think that we would all in turn take our place as Kingly, up there in the skies of cyber world.

We drew lots to see in which order we would become Kingly. Luke was to go first, followed by Katie, then Ed, and finally me. I didn't mind, I was strangely superstitious, and quite pleased to go last. I would be able to learn from the others' experience, and there was something rather thrilling about prolonging the suspense.

At last it was my turn. The others were all talking at once, saying how fantastic it was soaring high up in the sky. We had all been on the cyber world flight simulators, in planes and helicopters, and I guess deep down we were all a bit anxious that this would not be much different. Still, if what the others were saying was anything to go by, this was in a totally different league. I certainly wasn't going to be disappointed.

Ed finished unhooking the final connections to the game and laid them down ready for my turn. The adrenalin was pumping a steady rhythmical thump in my head. I felt rather nervous as I fumbled to put on the virtual reality headgear, and then attached the micro sensors into all key ports of my cyber suit. When I was ready I clicked on the flashing gateway icon, the screen melted away, and I was transported into the cyber world gateway; a sort of virtual waiting-room-cum-departure-lounge. I was asked to give the identification code of our clone, Kingly, and the transport tag code for the level 1 practice arena. After what seemed like an age, and could only have been a matter of seconds, I was given the all-clear. I was now authorised to enter the virtual transformer bay. I slowly entered the holding room of cyber world where the boundaries between virtual and real were blurred. It was here that I was going to transform into Kingly. Beyond this I would have no contact with the real world: all my senses and everything that I thought of as me, would now be as an eagle.

It was the most fantastic and weird sensation ever, something that would always give you that tingling feeling down your spine and butterflies in your stomach. No matter how many times I transformed into Kingly in the future I always had that strange tickling frisson of excitement. It never diminished.

I could feel the cool air lifting me off the ground and sense the power in my wings. I was amazed at how natural it all felt, as if I had always been able to fly. The wonderful free-falling sensation, like diving into water. Then, just as you were about to enter the water, pulling up and soaring into the skies. I felt powerful, with limitless energy and, above all, invincible. I swooped and dived around the practice arena. Gliding above the trees, and then weaving in between them, I was starting to feel confident. I knew that I now needed to start scoring points. I had to take on some of the game's pre-programmed clones in the practice arena. I circled around, savouring the mixture of thrill and fear as I focused on my first target – an unsuspecting stag. Even from my height I could see that it had an incredible pair of antlers, and as I got closer I could see the razor sharpness of their edges, a neat gene modification. I was thankful for my soundless flight. I would swoop down, make a gouge with my talons on his back, and get out as fast as my wings could take me. That should score a few points. I had a momentary hesitation, then dived at full speed with my talons outstretched. I was so close that I could feel the heat coming from the stag's body, and sense the rush of air pass over his coat from my wings. Suddenly, he turned on me and with a deafening grunt lunged his antlers towards me and bared his teeth. They were definitely not the teeth of a deer. The antlers clipped the edge of my wing feathers as I turned to fly away. I waited, but didn't feel any pain; I had escaped the strange grunting beast below, but had I scored any points? I circled around the treetops and looked down. There for all to see was the mark left by my talons. I had done it, but I wasn't going to hang around and see who else turned up on the scene. I had this strange emotion of complete fear and exhilaration. I knew that to succeed I had to stay and complete a fight to the end, but whose end would it be?

I felt as though I had been in this unreal world forever. I circled the arena several times and left my mark on a number of clone creatures. I suffered a couple of injuries, but they were minor, just a few displaced feathers. Then I saw what I was looking for: a solitary clone resting in the undergrowth. It looked like it might have been recently injured and was recovering. There was no time for sympathy, this was not that kind of game. It was about surviving, and winning at all costs. The clone was not large, some kind of feral cat. A bird and a cat, not generally a good combination when you're a bird, but then I was no ordinary garden variety of bird. I did a tight circle in the air, and swooped down low, startling the cat clone. I felt my talons scrape through the flesh and fur. I gripped hard, and tried to take off. My intention was to pick up the clone, mark it, and deposit it in the nearby lake. Unless they had modified a gene for swimming, most cats would flounder in the middle of a lake, which would make me an outright winner in the battle. I should have realised, however, that this was no ordinary cat. This clone had the teeth of a sabre tooth tiger and retractable claws that made my talons look like toy accessories. This was going to be harder than I imagined. I had merely wounded rather than stunned the cat when I picked it up: a serious error. I now had a razor-wielding machine writhing in my talons, trying to snap at my legs. I knew I was in trouble, and for the first time began to feel tired. The clone sensed this and started to taunt me.

"Feather-headed no-brain, had a manicure lately?" it hissed at me.

I had no choice, I had to carry on. I could see the lake up ahead. The clone started to writhe more earnestly now, making bold swipes at my wings and legs. I could feel my talons losing grip, but there were only a few more metres to go. I had to hang on. I felt a searing pain in my right leg and sensed blood trickling down. I hadn't realised how real the pain would be as a virtual clone. The burning sensation was unbearable, I just wanted to land and make it all go away. Then I learnt my most important lesson, one that was to be invaluable to me in cyber world. When you become your clone you are not merely taking over some other creature's body, you become them. Your mind is their mind, totally entwined, and the most powerful thing is the power of the mind, the control of the will over the physical body. If I felt defeated, then I surely would be…I had given in. If I knew I was invincible and could succeed, even against improbable odds…then I could. I needed to believe in myself. With a loud screech that startled even myself I found a new lease of energy. Soon I was circling over the lake and was able to let my unfortunate passenger free. The splash and yowl below me made it all worthwhile. I had won my first battle, the first of many to come, and in some ways the hardest. At last I made my way back to the cyber world gateway and into the transformer bay.

As I was unplugging the port cables from my cyber suit I could sense the others chatting animatedly.

"That was incredible," I managed to say at last.

It was a strange sensation. If I thought it was odd going from boy to bird clone in a virtual world, it was even weirder coming back. On leaving cyber world I had checked Kingly in with the clone vet, and I was assured that there was very little damage. This was good news on two counts. First, none of us could stand the thought of Kingly being hurt; even if he was virtual, he was real enough to us and indeed was a part of all of us. Secondly, and perhaps more importantly in terms of the game, it cost you hard-earned points to get your clones fixed.

I struggled to work out how the others knew so much about my flight as Kingly. That was until Katie confessed that they had all entered as spectators. They felt that considering I was last, and I wouldn't know, then it didn't really matter. This was true and in many ways worked in my favour. They were all agreed that I was to be the main "flier" as Kingly. We would all continue to practice, but I would compete in the competition, based on the number of points I had scored in the practice arena. I was naturally thrilled. I felt a strange dual personality: James the boy, and my alter ego, Kingly the eagle. How much is one part of the other? I bent down to rub my leg. I could have sworn that it felt like I had a scratch, but nothing was there, the skin was unblemished.

THE CHOSEN ONE

At last the day came when the winner of the schools competition was going to be announced. We had worked hard canvassing on behalf of Kingly. There couldn't be a single person across the school who hadn't heard of our clone. We also had the advantage that we were mentioned in the practice rounds bulletin board. Our names had been pasted up on the chat room board; we were up there as promising newcomers, and were to be watched. It couldn't have been better

Then the ultimate happened, more than we dared dream of. We were all gathered in front of the large screen, staring up at our illustrious headmaster, waiting for the announcement.

"Well," he said, "I am extremely pleased with the quality and imagination that has been put into the creation of these clones. I also hear from the Biogenetics department that they have never had so many requests for extra tuition. No doubt you will all score high in the end-of-year bioengineering exams. A rather fortunate spin-off from the competition." The headmaster paused for effect. "We have footage from the Animal Clones practice arena of the three finalists. Mr Hank, if you please…" The headmaster nodded over to the head of communications, Mr Hank, known affectionately as Ranky Hanky because of his unfortunate habit of picking his nose in public. I thought gene modification would have got rid of all those nasty habits by now.

The screen went blank, then the distinctive logo, "Animal Clones – The Battle of the Beasts," appeared. There was an audible intake of breath as the logo melted away into the now familiar scene of the practice arena. There up on the screen was Kingly. We had made it into the final three. We waited to see the other two contestants. Predictably, Heskins (owner of the highest IQ score in the school) and his cronies had their clone up on the screen as well. I have to say it was an impressive looking wolf-like creature. It certainly looked like it had undergone more than the standard three gene modifications allowed. Mind you, with their knowledge of gene interactions they probably could have done the impossible and changed a fish into a bird. Finally, the last clone to appear on the screen was a massive, evil-looking spider. It was really cool, it was almost a blur moving so fast, and its fangs were pure evil. That would be a tough opponent.

It was time to vote. As we filed out of the huge assembly hall, we all cast our votes at the fingerprint recognition pad. One press for Kingly, two for the Wolf, and three for the Spider. I was very nervous and worried about the sensitivity of the touch pad – had I managed inadvertently to vote for the opposition? I needn't have worried. We won by a comfortable majority. Obviously our campaigning had been worthwhile, but not only that, we now knew that others also believed in Kingly. I went around for the rest of that day with my head in the clouds. It really was a dream come true.

7

HELP FROM THE EXPERTS

Much to our surprise the teachers seemed impressed, and believe me it takes a lot to impress our teachers. Our head of technology, old Dobbo (well, Dr Dobson was his real name), said he was keen to help us and arranged for us to meet him straight after school in the technology suite. So there we were just after four o'clock, sitting among a large number of half-finished robots – a final-year project.

"Look at that one over there," said Ed, pointing at the most incredible-looking robot. It had four arms on a rotating torso with each arm having a number of gadgets attached. You know, everyday essentials, such as a long blade knife, a small blade knife, an incredibly pointed knife, serrated scissors or were they shears, and something that looked like a circular saw.

"Do you think that guy likes cutting things?" asked Luke.

"That's Charlie's sort of robot," I said, thinking of my younger brother.

"Glad you could make it," boomed a voice from behind us, as old Dobbo entered from the technicians' room. I didn't realise we had any choice in the matter, but wasn't about to voice this particular thought.

"Yes, sir, thank you for your time," we all chorused.

"You're probably wondering what an old has-been technology researcher turned teacher can do to help you young technical geniuses..." he started, giving each of us his uncomfortable intense stare. Oh no. You could almost hear our collective inward groan. Predictably he was going to head off on one of his long rambles, along the lines of when I was a young researcher doing my doctorate... Sure enough, we heard the familiar beginning, but just when we were all going into collective shutdown, he said something to make us switch on again.

"So, as I was saying, working in the labs at the same time was Professor Franklin, not that he was well known then. No, quite the converse, considered a bit eccentric with his gene modification theories. But we had shared interests in virtual robotics, a hobby of his and mine, and we became very good friends. In fact, we still keep in touch, though he must be well into his hundreds now. After all, he would have been seventy then," continued old Dobbo, smiling to himself.

Everyone knew Professor Franklin, who had become a public figure when he was game advisor for Clone Wars in the early days. Apart from his serious scientific books, he had written a number of gene modification strategy books for aficionados of Clone Wars. He was many a game-player's hero, even though the books were well above most of our heads. However, although the books remained classics, nothing much was heard about Professor Franklin these days. I have to say that I thought he was dead.

"If you all agree, I could arrange for you to meet Prof Franklin to talk strategy," said old Dobbo, fixing me with his gaze.

"Yes, yes, that would be great, really helpful…" I gabbled enthusiastically, knowing that I was safely speaking for all of us. We all sat there like a convention of nodding dogs.

I don't know how he sorted it, but as promised the next week we were at the laboratories of Professor Franklin. It was not quite the meeting of minds we had hoped for. He was clearly distracted, and appeared to be against the whole Animal Clone Wars thing.

"I'm not convinced about this schools competition, youngsters dabbling in what they don't understand, they'll have them deciding gene policy next. Still, can't be much worse than the fools doing that now. I've said for years that perfection isn't the answer. Anyway, who is to say what is normal and what is perfect? Ridiculous," rambled the Professor to no one in particular.

"Now, now Franklin old chap, you know you don't mean all that," said Dobbo, placing a hand on the Professor's shoulder. "It is important for these students to develop their genetics knowledge, after all our whole society revolves around it these days. Besides, it's good to have a lighter side with games such as Animal Clone Wars."

"I know, I know, but what worries me is that things may have gone too far. We need to respect nature and accept our limitations," replied the Professor wearily, taking off his glasses and sitting down. He cast his old eyes round us. What was he going on about? We hadn't come along for an ethical debate – had his mind gone?

"I'm sorry, I'm afraid I have become a bitter old man. The world was quite different when I was your age, and I find it hard to accept that it's partly my research that has pushed us into this world obsessed with gene perfection.

I thought by controlling our genes that we could alter our destiny for the better. I couldn't see any limitations of gene modification. I, too, thought the ultimate goal was to seek perfection." The Professor paused, and let out a long sigh before continuing.

"But now, I don't know anymore. I don't really know what perfection is anymore."

We exchanged looks, shuffled our feet, and looked with embarrassment at the floor. Maybe the old Professor had really lost it, perhaps even with drugs and gene therapy senile dementia had crept up on him. I was wondering what we were doing there, why had old Dobbo brought us here, did he not realise the state of the Professor? Then suddenly the Professor seemed to snap out of it.

"Enough of my morose behaviour. I have the opportunity to educate some fine young minds here into the art, because it is an art with just a hint of science, of gene modification strategy. But seriously, there is one thing I must ask you to agree with before I help you. You must agree to stop and think about what you are taking away with every gene modification, rather than what you might be trying to gain. Look at the whole picture, not just one side. Do you promise?"

We all said yes, though at the time it seemed a rather trivial thing for the old Professor to be asking us. It was only much later that we realised the importance of what he had said, and that he wasn't just talking about our Clone War games. The importance of thinking about the consequences before you start rather than when it is too late to go back, was an important lesson.

We had so much to learn, and learn we did. Professor Franklin was surprisingly coherent and interesting once he got going on gene modifications. He spoke with a passion and enthusiasm we rarely came across in our everyday schooling. The only thing more surprising was that we more than matched it with our own enthusiasm to learn. It was hard to imagine how we had managed to create our clone and get into the competition with so little knowledge between us. Now things would be different. If we made it through the qualifying rounds then we would be in a much better position to decide on our gene modification strategy. The key certainly was to think about the whole picture. We had to consider the combination of gene modifications that we would carry out, think about the ultimate creature we wanted to create, rather than getting easily sucked into the immediate effect syndrome, just to win the first round. It was valuable advice, and I knew it would work well for us. Fortunately, we hadn't carried out any irreparable damage with any early extreme gene modifications. Subtlety and gene interaction were the important lessons.

QUALIFYING ROUND

Over the next few days I spent hours in the practice arenas, and was beginning to feel more at ease with my virtual reality headgear. But was it enough? Then came the moment of truth, our qualifying round. Even though this was the real thing I calmly attached the micro sensors to my cyber suit, and then clicked on the gateway icon. As usual the screen melted away and once more I was transported into the now-familiar cyber world gateway. I entered Kingly's identification code followed by the transport tag code for the qualifying battle arena. To my surprise the virtual transformer bay was no different from the one used for the practice arena. I hoped that was going to be my only disappointment. My previous calm gave way to nerves, but I knew this would fade away as I took on the form of Kingly, the strange blur between the real and the virtual. It was just as I imagined the old-fashioned comic-book heroes to feel, the glorious transformation from human to super-being. As Kingly I could do anything.

The arena was sinister. It was the Wasteland, one of the hardest of the battle arenas. Why couldn't we have got something less threatening, like the City? This arena reminded me of the old post-nuclear holocaust films, all devastation, destruction and a lot of orange dust swirling around. Everywhere seemed deserted and extremely bleak. I was having difficulty dealing with the swirling dust and the unnatural glare bouncing off piles of metal scrap. Eventually my eyes adjusted and my superbly acute vision allowed me to scan the arena carefully. I had to make sure that I didn't become a sitting target; without any treetops or buildings I was vulnerably exposed in the sky. The silence was eerie. Even my own silent flight was disturbing.

Suddenly I detected some movement, or thought I had. Perhaps I was mistaken? No, I needed to trust in Kingly's instincts, switch off my own doubt and let the clone in me take over. I took another closer swoop down, not too low to allow an attacker to strike but low enough so that I could check out my opponent. Instinct was right. There among the glistening steel something was moving, but what? I upgraded my vision momentarily, requiring a lot of effort and concentration. I caught the glint of a hard black shell, the armoured casing of some sort of beetle. One gene modification was clearly visible, it was enormous. But I was confident, perhaps too confident. I thought with my powerful beak and talons, the bug would be no match for this eagle, I would simply peel him open like a tin of tuna. I circled, fixed my vision, locked on target and dived. My modified wings took me at a fearsome speed to my target. Just as I neared the ground, I swooped up, talons out, and took hold of the beetle's casing. I felt a horrible scraping and a searing pain in my right talons. The exoskeleton of this beetle had definitely been upgraded by a gene modification, and my ordinary eagle talons were useless against it. My outside right talon was badly injured, the impact had sent a nasty crack up its whole length. The pain was indescribable. I soared back up into the air seeking refuge in a newly formed cloud of dust. Why hadn't we modified Kingly's beak or talons? They were the obvious weapons. Why had we tried to be so clever with our strategic modifications? I felt I needed sheer brute-force weaponry at this moment in time. Still, I was safe for the time being up here in the cloud, or so I thought. I heard a deafening whirring noise, a cross between a helicopter and an old traction engine. I turned just in time to see that beast of a bug coming straight up into the air, with a fearsome pair of pincers heading for my underside. Instinct took over. I circled fast and, switching to my most powerful flight, I left the creature as if standing, in mid air. Surely I had seen all of this clone's gene modifications: size, super-toughened exoskeleton, and those awesome pincers. I had to think of what could be its weakness, but from where I was I couldn't see any obvious ones. One thing for sure, I certainly wasn't going to make it through this qualifying round by just flying away. I had to attack to gain points, and at the moment this flying bug was getting the better of me. I needed to tune in to Kingly's superior strategic brain. Surely we could outwit this overgrown garden beetle.

The beetle had settled again among the metal and debris, no doubt conserving its energy, perhaps it was very hard for it to maintain flight for long. Perhaps I could entice it into the air, give it a chase around, and attack when it flopped exhausted to the ground. There were just two flaws with that plan. Firstly, it probably wouldn't be so stupid as to fly until it dropped. And secondly, if it did, then I had no means of getting through that reinforced steel outer casing. At last a plan emerged, somewhat crazy to my mind as James, but a perfect strategy for Kingly. Now I put it into action. I swooped down, teasingly close to the beetle clone – if I misjudged it I would receive another injury from those powerful pincers. It was perfect. I could feel the air stir round my talons as the pincers lunged. As I headed back into the sky, I heard the whirr as the beetle took off from the ground. I had tempted him to attack. I just had to remain calm now, and delay switching on my powerful flight. I needed him to get up close before I could go for an attack. Just as he was getting close, I turned, switched to powerful flight, and using my precise vision focused on the soft exposed flesh beneath the hard casing of wings. In a flash I had him, my beak caught the soft flesh and, oozing a horrible black liquid, the beetle fell from the sky like a stone. Against all odds, Kingly's strategy had won the battle. We had won this qualifying round. I was lucky this time, but I had to learn to let go more, and let Kingly's mind take over. I knew that eventually I had to become completely Kingly, and my persona would no longer exist in the arena. It could no longer be we, I had to become him. I had little choice.

That night we were busy celebrating, and avidly discussing the next gene modifications we could make having won this qualifying battle. We had two more battles, and only had to win one to go into the next round. The others were getting very excited.

"Come on James, cheer up, anyone would think that Kingly had lost rather than won," said Luke, putting his arm around my shoulder.

I could see Ed watching me rub my right leg. He could sense that I was worried.

It had to be psychological. How could an injury sustained as a virtual clone trouble me in the real world? There was something disturbing about this. I was momentarily concerned about becoming part James, part Kingly the clone. It wasn't possible. I shrugged my shoulders.

"Sorry, I'm miles away, still lost in battle I guess," I said.

"Bit nerve-racking that one, clearly Kingly was short of attacking power. I think we should use our next gene modifications to sort that," said Ed.

We all agreed that this would be the most logical step.

The next few days were spent discussing the battle and contemplating the effects of our suggested gene modifications. Each of us took turns back in the practice arena as Kingly, to develop new battle strategies. Just as we were sitting around having one of our many discussions, Katie came running in looking rather agitated.

"Guys, just look at this. What do you think it's all about?" said Katie, thrusting her Tipdat into my face.

"Katie, my eyes can't possibly focus at that distance, what is it?" I asked.

"Well, can't you see?" she demanded, forcing the screen into Luke's face instead.

"Katie, calm down, just tell us," said Ed, reaching over to take the Tipdat.

Katie took a deep breath and began.

"I was just checking our Kingly site mail, and among the usual good-luck messages and battle suggestions was this one." Katie reached over and retrieved the Tipdat from Ed and began reading.

"A word of friendly advice. For your own good, stay away from Prof Franklin. There are things that are safer not known."

AN INVITATION WE COULDN'T REFUSE

If anything was going to make us curious it was a warning like that. The next day we headed over to old Dobbo's place and showed him the mail.

"How strange, how very strange," he murmured to himself, while plugging the Tipdat into his computer station. After a minute of furious tapping at his terminal, he paused, looked up, and sighed.

"That mail came straight from one of the terminals in Prof Franklin's lab. I think we ought to go back there and find out what's going on. He's been acting a little strange lately. But I can't believe that he's involved in anything bad."

Old Dobbo looked troubled. I was sure that he had a bad feeling about all this. I certainly had.

At the lab we were met with a friendly reception, much the same as we had become used to recently. Perhaps there was some big misunderstanding? Maybe someone was having a joke? But immediately Dobbo confronted Professor Franklin, I knew something was seriously wrong by the expression on his face. He seemed to age another hundred years in those few seconds.

"You'd better come with me," he said, gesturing towards his office. He turned and called over to a young researcher, one of his doctoral students.

"Ann, you'd better come in as well. I know it was you who sent the mail."

The girl flushed red, opened her mouth to say something, and then thought better of it. She put down the pipette she was holding, and walked slowly over. We all entered his office and he closed the door behind us.

"I'm not sure where to start. Perhaps we should ask Ann to begin, find out what she thinks is the danger," he said, turning to look at Ann.

She moved uncomfortably in her chair, and then began.

"I stand by what I did, I was worried and wanted to warn these kids not to get involved," she said defiantly. Then she seemed to soften visibly before continuing.

"I was worried about you too, Prof. I saw those men come into your office. It was a few weeks ago when I was working late. I was round over in the radiation lab, and I had forgotten one of my samples, so I came back to the main lab to collect it. But just as I was about to enter, I heard raised voices, and saw two men push you into your office. I should have confronted them, but I admit I was scared when I recognised one of them. My brother works for the Ministry of Mistreatment of Gene Modifications as an undercover investigator. I had seen that man on his computer screen, I know he is wanted in connection with serious gene violations. But there was something else familiar about him. I had seen him somewhere else, too."

"Clone Wars," interrupted the Professor.

"Yes, he was the scientist who had been caught rigging the early games. At first I couldn't understand why he was visiting you, then I remembered you had worked on the Clone Wars game. So you must have known him from the past. I hoped that you weren't involved in anything awful, but there just seemed too many coincidences. Whatever, I thought these kids would be better off staying out of it." Ann finished speaking, and looked the Professor straight in the eye as she waited for an explanation. But before he could answer, Dobbo spoke out.

"Prof, tell me this can't be true. I wondered why you left the game so abruptly. I thought it was because of the disagreement with the programme controllers. What does it all mean? You of all the people I have ever known, have been the most principled. I can't believe it."

All this time Professor Franklin sat there calmly. It seemed an age before he replied.

"I wish I was, I really wish I was. I guess we all have our price, and our principles change to suit us. But it is not quite as it seems. I think I had better start from the beginning. As ever, your impeccable logic was right, Ann. It was Dr Kirkland that you saw that night. He may have been discredited, but he wasn't the only one involved in rigging the competition. He was probably the most junior of those involved, and was a convenient scapegoat. Ironically, that probably forced him to become the criminal that he is today. I had realised some time before it was made public, that everything wasn't what it seemed, but I had already made the decision to leave. I didn't want to get involved, and Dr Kirkland certainly got what he deserved. I had no regrets about leaving. It had been fun working on the game, but I had serious research to pursue. My gene modification research. After all, I had my vision of perfection to chase." He let out a little bitter laugh, and then continued.

"I gave it no further thought. I couldn't afford to be associated with game rigging. Perhaps I should have told people what I had seen, perhaps then the people masterminding the rigging would have taken the blame, and perhaps even Kirkland might not have gone as far as he has. Who knows? At the time I didn't think I should get involved. I didn't want any complications. After all, my research was going well, I had a happy family life, and an extremely intelligent and beautiful daughter, my pride and joy. What more could I want? I felt that nothing could go wrong. The years went by, my research continued to flourish, my daughter got married and had her own family." Professor Franklin paused, momentarily lost in private thought. We all looked at each other, exchanging puzzled glances. Nothing seemed that awful. Okay, I guess he should have stood up and pointed the finger of blame. Then again, many of us ignore things so that we don't get involved. The old Professor could see that we were wondering where all this was going. He continued.

"I can see you are puzzled, but I do need to explain how everything unfolds from my seemingly privileged life. Going back to my story, you see at that time there was no sign of the devastation to come later. We were all considered so perfect, an excellent gene stock. Who could have guessed? My poor darling granddaughter, Grace. I remember her birth so clearly, and how proud I was on her wedding day. I thought I was the luckiest man alive when she announced she was expecting a baby, a little girl, to be called Lily. All the tests were carried out, and just as everyone expected, she was perfect. There was no need to tweak her genes, no gene modifications were necessary, or so we thought. Then, a short while after she was born, it became apparent that something was wrong. Baby Lily kept getting chest infections, something unheard of nowadays, and she wasn't feeding very well. I had my suspicions, but couldn't believe it. I secretly did a quick genetic test, and my fears were confirmed. Lily had cystic fibrosis, a single gene defect that has virtually been irradicated these days. After all, it is routinely checked for on the fetal genome scan. But why hadn't it been detected, why hadn't it been corrected? I am afraid we will never know. We could hardly make a fuss. If we did then the gene regulation authorities would be told that we had a child with an illegal gene defect."

"I'm sorry, Professor, but I don't quite understand. Why is it illegal? It wasn't your fault," interrupted Ed.

"I'm afraid it is nothing to do with who is to blame. It is about keeping the gene pool as pure and free of mutations as possible. That is the sole aim of the gene regulation authorities. Let me explain. Way back at the beginning of the 21st century scientists made a major breakthrough in genetics, they sequenced the entire Human Genome, and from that we now have the complete instructions to make a human being. Not only that, we were then able to identify all the mutations and changes in the DNA that made people ill. When I was working on this, we all thought it was wonderful. We were sure that we would be able to cure everyone, that it would be the end of genetic diseases and horrible deformities. Everyone would be perfect, well almost. It worked, mostly. First we tackled some of the simpler genetic disorders, moving on to more complex ones. Then we wanted to do the ultimate: to change genes before a baby was born, ensuring that everything was perfect. We should have known that this could be taken too far, and it has been – even the slightest genetic imperfection is now frowned upon. We have changed the boundaries of what is accepted as normal in society. Like many others in history before us, we were only trying to do what we thought was the right thing. We wanted to stop suffering not create more anguish." The Professor paused, checking our faces to see if we had followed him. We had, it was all too clear.

"Ah," he went on, "I suppose many would say I have got my just reward. But let me tell you of my granddaughter, and poor unfortunate Lily. I'm sure you all realise that before you can have children you must undergo a genetic profiling test and obtain a breeding certificate. Well, that was fine, and the embryo, to be my great-granddaughter, was produced and checked at the Genetic Control Centre. It is at this stage that minor gene defects can be corrected or gene enhancements can be carried out. My granddaughter certainly didn't want to enhance any of her child's genes and was happy to be told that everything was fine. Clearly, we know now it was not. We will never know whether the error was deliberate or not. It's even possible that someone actually introduced the mutation."

"Surely that couldn't possibly happen?" interrupted Katie.

"I'm afraid there have been cases of disgruntled workers, who are not allowed to have children themselves, taking revenge on others who are. But this is all irrelevant now. What I needed to do was cure my little great-granddaughter. I had to get access to old-fashioned gene therapy. I should explain that this was the way we used to correct faulty genes in the past, long before we had the ability to change genes in the unborn child, in the fetus. In these old cases we had to try to correct the faulty gene once the disease had taken hold. Sometimes damage had already been caused by the faulty gene and it was too late. However, the faulty cystic fibrosis gene was a good target for that kind of gene therapy, and the faulty gene could be replaced with the correctly working gene in the tissues that were most affected, in this case the lungs. So there was still a chance for Lily, but I had to do it quickly before anyone found out. As I said, it is illegal to knowingly have a child with a genetic defect and my granddaughter, Grace, would be in danger of having her breeding licence taken away. Worse still, Lily would be reduced to clone status. Both their lives would be destroyed. I just had to do something. The trouble was it is all very expensive and actually difficult to get hold of the equipment and materials for the old gene therapy methods. If people found out it would raise suspicions. I was desperate. I knew that one person would be able to help, but at a price."

"Dr Kirkland?" whispered Ann.

"Yes, he was able to provide me with everything I needed. But there was a price to pay. He needed some help with a new underworld game of Clone Wars. Not virtual, but real live clones. Clearly totally illegal. He wanted my help to create the ultimate battle clone. I didn't think of the conse-quences. I never seem to. I needed to cure Lily, so I agreed to his terms. The trouble is now I am involved too far. I have helped him with his battle clone, but he wants more. If I don't continue I run the risk that he will inform the gene reg-ulation authorities about Lily. I can't take that risk. I should never have trusted him, but desperate men take desperate measures. So you see now, why they were paying me a visit last week. They wanted me to do some more work." The Professor stopped talking and sank back into his chair. He looked even older than his many years, if that was possible.

"I'm so, so sorry Professor, but surely there must be some way of sorting this out. You can't let Kirkland get away with this, " said Ann.

"I see now why you were reluctant to help with the com-petition. Rather a mess isn't it?" said Old Dobbo.

"Master of the understatement as ever," retorted Professor Franklin, sitting back up in his seat and managing to half-raise a smile.

"What happens now?" I asked nervously. "I mean, surely Dr Kirkland isn't interested in us or the Animal Clones competition? After all, these are just regular virtual clones made by school kids."

"I'm afraid you are wrong. Dr Kirkland is extremely wealthy, and he didn't get that from being a mediocre scientist. You remember I said he was dismissed from the original Clone Wars competition because of rigging? Although he was very junior in that particular case, he has progressed to become a truly brilliant career criminal in the underworld. Apart from his illegal real clone battles, he has masterminded the rigging of many competitions since. He most certainly will have an interest in the Animal Clones competition, and I am sure he is already working out how to make money from it. You must remember that he is always looking for an opportunity to make money and has no morals regarding how he goes about it. He won't think twice about this being a children's competition. If humans can be truly evil, then he is. Nothing crosses any boundaries for him." Professor Franklin looked grim.

"But the prize money isn't that much," said Luke.

"No, if he has an interest it won't be the actual prize money that he is after, it will be the betting on the individual clones and on the outcome of each battle. A lot of money is exchanged. It is illegal of course, but it is well known to be a favourite pastime of the worker clones. The authorities turn a blind eye to it. "

At that moment the door opened and there, silhouetted in the frame, stood the infamous Dr Kirkland. My heart took a leap into my throat as my stomach descended. After the initial shock I thought that perhaps he didn't look that scary, just sort of creepy. But there standing behind him were his two mountains of henchmen. I bet they were modified battle clones. One thing was for sure, none of us were about to argue or risk a fight.

I glanced at the others. They looked as uncomfortable as I felt.

"So good to see you encouraging youngsters, Franklin. I do think it is very important to catch them young. Their minds are so much easier to influence, and after all we do need to shape the scientists of the future," said Dr Kirkland in a slow easy drawl.

"What is it you want, Kirkland? Can't you see I am busy?" snapped Professor Franklin.

"Just a little social call to invite you to witness the new battle clone. I think it needs some more modifications, so you need to see it in a real battle," continued Dr Kirkland.

"You know I don't like watching those things in action," mumbled the Professor, almost to himself.

"Well, at least this time you will have your young companions to hold your hand. After what I've just heard, I insist that they come with you. You know how much I value education. Besides, it would be most unfair for them not to form their own opinions. " He smiled, the lazy, self-satisfied smile of a reptile, and turned to leave. As he reached the door he put up his hand to his henchmen to stall them and turned back. "Don't worry, I'll arrange for my men to collect you."

10

THE UNDERWORLD

There seemed to be no way we could get out of it and the following week, true to his word, Dr Kirkland sent his henchmen to collect us from Prof Franklin's office. We were then taken to the private underground laboratories of his company, Genecon. He was waiting for us in his plush office.

"So glad to see you all again," he smarmed, almost pleasantly. Why did he always remind me of a reptile?

"Now, I'm afraid that I have to keep our location a secret, for security reasons you understand, so I apologise for the basic nature of our transport." And with that he left the room. We were herded behind him by his henchmen and led down to a large underground chamber. In the centre was a state-of-the-art secure travel pod, the ones that were used by the security forces to escort dangerous criminals. Under slightly different circumstances I would have been excited to travel in the pod. I could see that Ed was trying to stifle his curiosity, and not ask questions about speed. The henchmen pushed us in, and secured the pod for travel.

Our actual destination was certainly a mystery, not even Professor Franklin knew exactly where we were going. Of course he knew the physical layout of the location, as that was necessary for him to design and modify Dr Kirkland's battle clone, but its whereabouts were kept secret. Apparently it was a small cluster of uncharted islands that had arisen after a massive volcanic eruption a number of decades ago. They were bleak, with a post-holocaust landscape, and were used by Dr Kirkland for illegal clone battles. These we had been warned were live battles, nothing virtual about these competitions.

Dr Kirkland was there to meet us.

"My dear friends, so glad you arrived safely. I trust your journey wasn't too uncomfortable?"

Katie was looking pale, the travel pods were not great if you suffered from motion sickness. Mind you, it would be difficult to say, looking round, who was feeling travel sick and who was just sick with worry.

"Now the excitement begins. You children will be able to see real genius at work. Yes, the old Professor has a real talent for genetic modifications, ironic considering his present predicament. You could have made a fortune if you had worked with me, Professor." Dr Kirkland gave us one of his smug reptilian smiles.

"Dr, sir, we must take up our positions before the battle begins." A small frog-like man had sidled up to Dr Kirkland and was trying to get his attention.

"Yes, yes, Dart, we are moving to the observation tower now," snapped Dr Kirkland impatiently. I couldn't help wondering how this Dart had managed to pass through the gene regulation checks. He certainly looked odd. I was sure his skin had a strange wet glow to it. I could see Luke staring as well. He caught my eye and started making quiet frog noises.

"I see you have spotted the amphibian gene modification in Dart, an early experiment, none too successful. I was hoping for the poison of a Dart frog. That would have been useful in a battle clone. Still, he has his uses," said Dr Kirkland dismissively.

I saw the creature, Dart, glance sideways at Dr Kirkland, a picture of resentment. I was sure any loyalty he showed was forced out of him rather than given willingly. Fear is a tremendous motivator.

The observation tower loomed out of the bleak landscape. You could see black volcanic rocks everywhere, evidence of the island's beginnings. Also, there were strange structures, clearly artificial features that had been introduced to make interesting battling arenas. I could feel the hair on my scalp prickling, this was a spooky place. Dart fussed around Dr Kirkland, making sure he had everything he wanted, while he kept glancing at us sideways with obvious disapproval. He clearly thought we shouldn't be there. I have to say, I was with him on that one.

"Now my young protégés, you are about to see some real battle clones, none of this imitation stuff, the so-called virtual reality. Watch closely and you'll learn," said Dr Kirkland.

"These children are no more your protégés than I am your partner in this dreadful business," said Professor Franklin angrily.

"Ha," laughed Dr Kirkland. "You do yourself down, Professor; we couldn't have achieved all this without your generous co-operation. But before we get into a round of mutual accolades, we must see the battle. You children can watch and learn. Perhaps you may get some ideas of how to fight with Kingly."

What did he know about Kingly? Had he really been watching our battles? He was beginning to make me feel even more uneasy than before. I remembered what Professor Franklin had said earlier about him being evil. I caught Ed giving me a sideways glance and saw he also looked troubled.

Below, the battle had now commenced. I could feel the tension in the room. None of us wanted to be here, apart from Dr Kirkland who was obviously enjoying himself, made all the better by our discomfort. The carnage below was horrific. There were four clones battling it out, not two on two, but three on one. The clones appeared to be variants on your classic werewolf. The bodily contortions were grotesque, and their obviously steel teeth and claws glistened eerily in the half-light of this bleak landscape. The only splash of colour was red, literally a liberal splattering of freshly spilt blood. A fifth clone appeared from the far side, emerging out of the shadows. It wasn't physically as big as the others but there was something else about it that made it stand out as something to be reckoned with. This was clearly Dr Kirkland's new battle clone, the one the Professor had been working on. Momentarily, I had to admire the sheer magnificence and horror of this beast. The three clones sensed its presence and turned to face their new contender, leaving the other clone in tatters on the floor. They seemed to go into pack formation, the leader at the front flanked by the other two at the sides. Teeth were bared and claws at the ready as they advanced, but they were no match for the lone battle clone, which clinically dealt with them, first one and then the other two. It was hard to believe that this was real. I have never before had such a sinking feeling in my stomach. I know that people say you can feel sick at the sight of things, but I always thought this was an exaggeration. Not any more. How had it come to this? What were we doing here? All of our dreams of the schools competition and the victory that could be ours, seemed childish and selfish. Below was a gruesome battle for life. All in the name of a game. I could see skin hanging in ribbons and fresh wounds seeping like burst over-ripe tomatoes. It was grim.

In a short while it was all over. As expected, Dr Kirkland's battle clone had won.

"I congratulate you Professor Franklin, a real victory for the new battle clone. The modifications were just right, as ever," said Dr Kirkland, turning to smile at the Professor, who was sitting very still with his head in his hands. At that moment he looked very small and old. Then Dr Kirkland turned his attention to us.

"I hope you are suitably impressed. I have let you into my little secret, now you must do something for me."

I didn't need to look up at the others to sense their dread. What was going to be our price? We never asked to get caught up in this, it just somehow happened.

"I know that Professor Franklin feels he has paid for his, what shall we call it, indiscretion or folly? I hope that his great-granddaughter was worth it. I never did ask whether the treatment was successful."

"Get on with it Kirkland, I don't need your false concern. What more do you want out of me, and why do you need to involve these innocent children?" snapped the Professor.

"Come, come Professor, of course I care, and most of all I care about the success of these children. All I want are some favourable odds on the schools competition. What better than inside information?"

"I'm sure it's not just information you want. After all, that isn't guaranteed to give you the outcome you want."

"I shouldn't underestimate you, Professor. A mere technicality, when I refer to information. Of course what I want from the children is a predicted outcome from the next round. That way I can influence the betting to my considerable advantage. I know that Kingly is an outsider, and I want to make sure that he remains that way, right until the very end. I need you, Professor, to oversee the gene modifications to ensure that Kingly is unbeatable; that is, unbeatable when I want him to be and not before. So the gene modifications you introduce should not be used until the final qualifying battle. It is good to have a few surprises, one should never reveal one's full hand at the beginning. After all, that shows our weakness, doesn't it, Professor?"

"But why should I help you with this?" demanded Professor Franklin.

"Well, I wouldn't think it was much to ask, a last farewell gift, a thank-you if you like, before we go our separate ways. After all I don't suppose you want any information leaking to the gene regulation committee just as everything is going through?" said Dr Kirkland, barely disguising his evil grin.

"But you can't make us do it," shouted Katie, feisty as ever.

Dr Kirkland slowly turned round to face us. The look on his face was like the one adults reserve for small children and animals. A pitying, superior look.

"My dear, you have little choice. In case your small brain hasn't registered, you are already in a big mess. Just imagine how the authorities would react if your names were linked with unseemly activities such as gambling, and then you were associated with the so-easily discredited Professor Franklin. It can be arranged." He turned back to the Professor.

"I want you to make the necessary gene modifications needed for the eagle clone to be invincible. And make sure that these good children are well practised in the battle arena. They need to look convincing losers, as well as knowing how to handle the gene modifications when it is time for them to win. I will be in touch with further instructions for you Professor, so the ball is in your court...or should I say the battle clone is in your arena?" He allowed himself a self-satisfied chuckle before continuing. "What a dilemma. Save your precious granddaughter from public humiliation, and your wretched great-granddaughter from a life as a lowly clone. Or you could be high and mighty and expose everything, including the involvement of these youngsters. Just think of the consequences you will face. Not to mention a few rounds in the arena with a battle clone – first-hand experience of your handiwork, though you probably wouldn't be in a position to make any last-minute adjustments." This clearly amused Dr Kirkland and he once again started to laugh that horrible, self-satisfied laugh of his. This was bad enough, but Dart had also started to laugh, a sickening hiccoughing laugh like a gurgling mud-clogged drain. My stomach fell past my knees. We were done for.

"How splendid, how terribly good, sir," slimed Dart between stifled hiccoughs, extending a slimy limb to con-gratulate the Doctor. Dr Kirkland swung round almost knocking Dart over.

"Remember, nobody touches me. Now get them out of my sight," he snapped nastily at Dart, standing up and striding across the room. He turned and fixed his cold glassy stare on the Professor.

"I will be in touch," he hissed.

11

GENE MODIFICATIONS

In a few days' time we found ourselves back in Professor Franklin's laboratory. Glumly, we all sat staring at the huge screen on the wall. We were looking at Kingly's genetic profile stored on the Professor's computer. The Prof was lost in deep thought, pondering the next gene modifications that would make Kingly unbeatable. It didn't seem right. We were misusing Kingly, corrupting our innocent clone; that is, if a virtual clone can be innocent or corrupt. I felt bad, but I couldn't help taking an interest in the Professor's work. I felt guilty about the excitement that was building up inside me. I really wanted to see how Kingly's new gene modifications would work, and was longing for the chance of a test flight. I tried to keep my curiosity and interest in check, but it was a losing battle. I couldn't help but notice that Luke and Ed were also intrigued. The Professor was muttering to himself as he worked.

"Mmmm, that should work, but perhaps not quite balanced enough. Subtle, subtle, we must be subtle…"

"Professor?" I asked quietly, not knowing whether to disturb him or not. My voice seemed to echo around the lab and come back to me, taking me by surprise. It seemed an age before he answered.

"Yes, yes, what is it?" he asked, not turning away from the keyboard on which he was tapping furiously.

"Will the gene modifications help Kingly attack?" I asked.

"We were thinking after the first qualifying round that we were a bit short on attacking power," said Ed.

"Yes, I think you're absolutely right. I have been looking at ways to enhance his fighting power. I'm sorry, I should have been discussing this with you as I've been working. But as ever, I got engrossed in the science. I must say that it has been a blessing to be taken over by the challenge. It has been a welcome relief from all the troubles. I hope you don't think badly of me doing this, but I can't help but do my best. This isn't just for Dr Kirkland. I'm not sure if you would understand, but it isn't in me to do mediocre science," said the Professor.

"It's okay, Professor, I think we do understand. Though perhaps in a different way. I think that we owe it to Kingly to do our best by him," replied Ed.

"I agree with Ed, we do owe it to Kingly," I added.

"Too right, we can't let our friend down," said Luke.

"All for one, and one for all, or something like that. Whatever, Kingly is our one and he deserves to be the best. Don't you agree, Professor?" asked Katie.

The Professor half smiled, and nodded. That was it, a cue for all of us to leave our guilt behind. The room was suddenly animated. Everyone was talking at once, offering the Professor advice on gene modifications. Not that he needed any, and he probably wasn't going to take any from us.

"Now, now, remember you don't have to keep thinking big. We can't go in all guns blazing. Subtlety is best. Not to mention vital, if we are to keep these gene modifications hidden from our opponent. You can't flaunt them in their face and expect them not to notice. An element of surprise is essential," cautioned the Professor.

By the end of the day numerous gene modifications had been tried. These had ranged from changing feather formation to aid flight, to enhancing different brain functions. We even managed to persuade the Professor to try some of our more extreme modifications, outrageous and totally unsubtle, just so that we could see what would happen. Of course he was right. Kingly looked like an extra from the set of a war film with oversized samurai sword talons and an overlapping shield of titanium feathers. Awesome, but he could barely fly. It was easy to see that there were no real beneficial effects from these modifications. Much more had been lost than gained. Still, it would have been quite something to try and take Kingly for a round in the practice arena like that. The Professor could clearly sense our thoughts.

"Sorry chaps, I know how tempting it is, but we really haven't got enough time. Besides, you'll get plenty of practice flights once I have authorised these final modifications. I'm almost there. Just one last tweak. Done," declared the Professor, sitting back in his chair. We gathered round to check out the new gene modifications.

They were quite something. First he had enhanced the power of Kingly's beak. It didn't look so different, but could now slice through metal. Mere flesh and bone would be no problem, not even toughened exoskeletons, should we come across another of those. The second modification was to his talons. He could now extend them with a twist and a flick, just like a blade shooting out of a flick knife. As the Professor had said, they were subtle. Kingly looked no different. These modifications would definitely have the element of surprise.

It had been a long day and we all agreed, with some reluctance, that it would be better to save the test flights for the next day. Despite the seriousness of our situation we went home that night on a high, the first time in a while. We had something to look forward to the next day, and we were going to hold on to that thought for just one night anyway. The problems and complications seemed almost as though they existed in a parallel world.

PRACTICE MAKES PERFECT

We were all still in a state of excitement the next day. Even the time lapse hadn't allowed us to dwell on darker things. We were avidly discussing the practice arenas, and which ones we wanted to test Kingly out on, when the Professor entered.

"Which practice arenas do you think would be best, Professor?" asked Ed.

"I'd like to go into the wasteland first," said Luke.

"Ahh, perhaps I haven't quite made this bit clear. I'm afraid that we can't go into any of the official practice arenas, that would be foolish at this stage, and would certainly upset Dr Kirkland," said the Professor.

"I don't understand. Why not?" I asked.

"Well, if we are to keep these gene modifications secret, a public practice arena that anyone can access is not such a good idea," said the Professor, looking much more serious than yesterday.

"So we won't be able to practise then?" asked Katie.

"Well, certainly not in the usual arenas. I have been giving this some thought overnight, and I'm afraid that my solution is far from ideal. I will explain it to you, but it is up to you if you don't want to go ahead. I will perfectly understand," said the Professor. This was ominous. Given the trouble we were already in, what could be worse? The Professor started to explain.

"When I was working as an advisor on Clone Wars, we had a lot of development work carried out on arenas. I'm talking a long time ago so I'm afraid they weren't that sophisticated. Well, I suppose that's not fair – they were for their day, but wouldn't seem it now. As more were developed and enhanced, older ones became obsolete and defunct. This was happening at an incredible rate. No one at the time wanted to delete the old arenas, after all we had a lot to learn and they provided a useful archive. That is until they became so many. At that time the cataloguing became less rigorous, and apart from those directly involved nobody really knew what still existed. There became a cyber junkyard of these virtual arenas, and they were mostly forgotten about. However, after a time there were rumours that cyber pirates were using these arenas – these are underground hackers who like to enter old decommissioned, but still classified, areas of the cyber world. There were suggestions that unofficial tournaments with illegal clones were taking place. We are still talking virtual clones here, not quite the horrors that Dr Kirkland is involved in. It rapidly became an aficionado's paradise. A challenge. There was a strange mixture of academics and pirates using the arenas in the cyber junkyard. You must remember there was raw excitement in these primitive places, excitement of a kind that had been lost in some of the more sophisticated arenas. I have used these places myself, many years ago, to test my gene modification strategies. But now, they have become just another dark place in the underground cyber culture."

The Professor paused to check that we were still with him.

He then went on to explain that these defunct arenas soon became the playgrounds of the criminal element of hackers, people with something to hide. Not really the place for your average virtual reality gamer. He suggested that we could test out Kingly's new modifications in such a place, but we needed to be aware that there were dangers. I guess at this moment we weren't so different from those rogue hackers, as we also had something to hide. However, the problem was that although the Prof could access the arenas, he wouldn't be able to have any control once Kingly had entered, and there wouldn't be any of the usual safety features of the official practice arenas. It was our decision.

"I will leave you to decide and I'll come back later. I'll be in my office if you need me." And with that the Professor turned and left.

We exchanged glances and I knew before the Professor had even left the room what our decision would be. We were unanimous. No matter what doubts we had, we were willing to take Kingly into one of these underground arenas. Our concept of danger was a bit vague after all that had happened recently. It was probably naïve, but we felt that no harm could come to us as Kingly.

"After all, it is just a virtual arena. It can't be so different from the others we've been in," said Katie.

"Yeh, what could possibly go wrong in there?" agreed Luke.

I wasn't so sure. I still remembered my mind playing tricks with the scratch on my leg from before: that pain had felt very real at the time. But while I was lost in my thoughts, Ed had already run off to tell the Prof our decision.

We now had a more important decision to make: the order for practice flights in the cyber junkyard arena. It was finally agreed that as the most experienced I should go first and report back to the others. It certainly wouldn't be sensible for any of us to enter as spectators in these places. If I felt threatened or unsure in any way I was to exit immediately. That's assuming I could, but I didn't like to mention that.

I felt a mixture of fear and excitement as I mentally prepared myself to enter. The Prof had selected an arena from the cyber junkyard, a former city arena. In its day it was a mock-up of historic New York, it even had the Twin Towers, which shows how ancient it was meant to be. He was now furiously tapping away at his terminal looking for the way in – the gateway opportunity for New York. I was ready with my virtual suit on, plugged into the computer. At a signal from the Prof, all the ports were to be switched to virtual and I would enter the unknown. I had the signal, no turning back now as the switches were flicked to virtual and I faded from the real world to my cyber destination. There were no fancy waiting rooms, niceties or gateway protocols to follow here. I appeared in what was a darkened tunnel. Surely I wasn't expected to transform here in the tunnel? Well, I certainly didn't want to stay here as James, that felt far too vulnerable. I glanced around looking for signs of a transformation bay. An electronic voice broke the silence making me jump. Not the pleasant tones I was used to, but a harsh electronic crackle.

"State your purpose," it demanded.

I wasn't sure whether to answer or not, but almost automatically I replied.

"I...I am here to practise in the cyber arena," I stammered in a small voice.

"State your purpose," repeated the voice.

Maybe it hadn't heard, perhaps it was ignoring me? What answer should I have given? Some kind of password? Panic welled up inside me; well, that is, a higher level of panic than my current baseline. Then I realised. The voice wasn't actually waiting for a reply, it wasn't even asking me a question. I had merely tripped a virtual beam that I could now see, and it must be linked to an automatic recording. This was probably the standard question asked of all entrants in the past, before the arena was defunct. By now I realised that I wasn't going to find anything that I would call a transformation bay. I stepped into one of the recesses in the tunnel walls. This was probably the best I was going to get. I knew that I was most vulnerable at the time of trans-formation and I felt the need to get out of the main tunnel. After all, psychologically and emotionally the transforma-tion point was where you left your human form. This was where James was to wait for me, even though I was really sitting back in the lab, in the real world, safely inside my cyber suit. Weird, I never could get used to this. I guess it was a common feeling, which was why the privacy of the transformation bays had been developed in the current cyber arenas. I nestled towards the back of the tunnel recess, making myself as small as possible.

As I transformed into Kingly I could feel my strength growing, along with my confidence. After all, Kingly's home was the cyber world. Now, completely transformed, I flew effortlessly to the end of the tunnel. It wasn't quite what I expected. There was an almost warm orange glow over a crowded skyline of tall buildings. Old-fashioned skyscrap-ers. I never did understand why they were called that. They certainly didn't scrape the sky, and were relatively small compared to today's standards. I recognised in the dis-tance the famous historical statue, what was it – The Statue of Liberty. That had been destroyed by terrorists a long time ago, a bleak period of history if I remember rightly, though history is not my strong point. I scanned the arena. Even I could tell that this was not the most sophisticated of cyber worlds. I could detect the edges, gaps where programming holes existed, rough patches in the code defining where one object finished and another started. These days you had seamless overlap. It was said that if you passed over one of these gaps while in cyber world you would disappear into a cyber no-man's-land, a place not even in the "real" virtual world. You would be lost forever, just another piece of computer code. I was always a bit sceptical of this, but right now I wasn't going to put it to the test. I didn't want to find myself trapped here forever. I made up my mind to stay away from those fuzzy edges and remain firmly within the main part of the programmed arena, which appeared to be functioning well despite its age.

I was somewhat surprised to find myself alone. Well, it suited me fine. I could take this chance to explore the arena fully, and check out Kingly's flying ability with the added weight of the new gene modifications. Although they were subtle, and you couldn't see the changes, I still noticed the heaviness in my beak and talons. It felt like a heavy dull ache to start with, but before long I had forgotten about it. I was soaring and swooping with the ease and grace I was used to. It was great to have that free feeling again, and already my anxiety had disappeared. I was starting to enjoy myself.

I needed to test out the new gene modifications. With a small twisting movement I was able effortlessly to snap out the blades from my talons. They were incredible, but I had to be careful as the extended length needed adjusting for. I swooped down to imaginary targets, judging my distance carefully and flicking out the blades at the last minute. I had a few scary moments when I found myself too close and almost ground to a halt, impaled on my target, but soon I had the hang of it. These were going to be very useful in battle. They would certainly come as a surprise to any opponent. I now had to try out the extra strength in my beak. I circled the arena looking for targets to mangle. I quickly sliced my way through building debris and scrap lying around. Nothing was a match for this beak, it really did cut through everything like a hot knife through butter. I was feeling very pleased with myself and was now putting together neat fighting sequences, diving down, attacking with my beak, gripping or slicing my imaginary target before triumphantly snapping out my talon blades to finish them off. I whooped and circled in a mock victory flight. I couldn't wait to tell the others about this.

Just as I was making light work of my next imaginary opponent, a voice startled me.

"Awesome, that is no ordinary gene modification. I haven't seen anything quite as sophisticated as that before. You're good, really good. Who are you?"

I turned but couldn't see where the voice was coming from. I changed my visual acuity to maximum and scanned again. There was a strange worm-like creature. It looked almost comical. Certainly no threat to Kingly. I landed on a building nearby, showing off with a fast dive and pulling up to dead stop in a flurry of dust.

"Thank you, have you been watching me for long?" I asked.

"Ohhh, so spectacular, so scary, can you show me again...please..." slimed the worm. I didn't need any more encouragement. I took off, executed a tight turn and at high speed dived towards the creature, flicking my talon blades in and out, just millimetres from its slimy skin.

"How was that, pretty good?" I boasted, knowing that I looked impressive.

"I...I...I'm still shaking with fear, please promise not to harm me," said the worm, shaking all over.

I laughed. "Sorry little chap, you're not my size. I only take on bigger creatures. It would be an unfair match," I said, relaxing my stand.

"I wouldn't be quite so sure if I were you, I am deadlier than I look, but I agree you would be an awesome opponent. Perhaps you would like a bit of sport with myself and a few of my companions?" said the worm, not sounding in the least scared or impressed anymore. I was confused. But before I could answer, the floor was covered in these gross little green worms. It was as if a blanket had been thrown down on the floor, and it was growing. Where were they coming from? I was beginning to be alarmed. Something wasn't right. Then I noticed that they were crawling out from the gaps in the programme. I realised these were no ordinary worms. These were the deadly programme worms that infected and destroyed all computer programmes. They were gradually increasing the size of the gap, expanding cyber no-man's-land, infecting and breaking down the arena. No wonder the arena had been empty. They had turned it into a desolate wasteland and were waiting to feast on any unsuspecting virtual creature that entered. I was surely a find, a sophisticated snack of programming, a real delight for their uneducated palate. I had to do something fast, but what? Surely I couldn't go near these creatures, just one of them infecting me would start to unravel my programme. I would fall apart, but what would happen to me as James in the real world? I didn't want to find out.

"Lost your appetite? Too many of us little unworthy creatures?" taunted the first worm.

They didn't look so comic now as they continued to pour out of the gap and crawl up the sides of the building on which I was perched. Presumably these things couldn't fly. I took to the only refuge I knew, the orange sky.

"How long can you stay up there? We can wait, no hurry. In fact it just increases my appetite," drooled the now grotesque worm.

I had to get back to the tunnel, transform back to James, and get myself out of this living nightmare. But these things seemed to be growing and multiplying by the minute. I was doomed.

At that moment, in the distance, I heard the automatic electronic voice.

"State your purpose," it demanded.

Had someone else entered this cyber arena? Maybe this would be my chance. But I couldn't fly over and check, not just yet. I needed to leave the tunnel area free of these worms for now. No use blocking my only exit route. I waited, glancing over to the tunnel entrance, switching my visual acuity back on to maximum. I knew I needed to conserve energy, but right now I needed to know if anybody was there and if they could help me.

It wasn't quite what I expected, although I'm not too sure what I did expect. But this was not a regular clone that I had come across in most virtual games. It was some strange robotic creature, equipped with sweeping nets and dragging behind what looked like numerous cages attached by chains. It made a strange sing-song sound as it moved.

"Coming to get you, coming to get you, come to Mummy..."

I wasn't sure what help a clanking, demented robot would be in a cyber junkyard. In fact it looked like it was made from the traditional scrap of a real junkyard. This was getting bizarre. I had been sufficiently distracted that I had absent-mindedly been lowering my circling flight. I was dangerously close to the buildings below. To my horror a number of the worm creatures launched themselves, kamikaze-style, towards me. A flick of my talon blades beheaded the nearest two as they dripped back to the ground. That was close, but I was worried that a mere speck of their programme on my talons might have infected me. Whatever that thing was down by the tunnel entrance, I had to head there.

As I moved, the sea of squirming green below followed me. It was like a tide moving up the shore. But almost as soon as it had started to move it stopped suddenly, a writhing mass piling up to make an absurd wriggling mountain. The front worms were trying to stop and turn round, while the back ones were blindly going forward. What had changed their minds? Then I realised, it was the weird robotic creature that they were afraid of. It continued towards them, singing as it moved.

"Coming to get you, coming to get you, come to Mummy…"

Its chains rattled eerily and it made large sweeps with its nets. I could hardly believe it. It was actually catching the worms and sticking them into the cages. The squealing and commotion intensified below, as worm scrabbled over worm to try and get back into the gap they had come from. I was mesmerised. All I could do was watch the strange scene unfold. Suddenly, I came to my senses. I had to get out of here. Now was my opportunity to make for the tunnel entrance and transform back to James before exiting this awful place.

I used the full power of my wings to get to the tunnel as fast as I could. My first panic was that I wouldn't be able to find the tunnel recess where I had transformed. I had an awful vision of James crawling with those disgusting green worms and never able to get back. Even though fear gripped me I carried on. In my panic I flew straight past the recess, realised, did a quick about turn and swooped back. At last, I hurled myself into the relative safety of the recess and began my transformation. The wretched electronic voice was ringing in my ears as I transformed.

"State your purpose," it repeated, fading in the distance.

I was back safely in the lab. By the look on the others' faces they had also been aware of what had happened in the cyber junkyard.

"Stay back, don't crowd him and don't get too close just yet. James, don't unplug the virtual reality suit. I still need you connected to the computer and Kingly," shouted the Professor, furiously working on the computer terminal in front of him.

My heart sank, something was wrong. What now?

"Okay, just a few more minutes and I'll have it," he barked.

It was the longest few minutes I have ever spent. It was as if time had stopped.

"Done, thank goodness for that," sighed the Professor, visibly relieved. "You and Kingly had a lucky escape there."

The Professor explained that a complication of these disused programmes in the cyber junkyard was that they were a breeding ground for worms and viruses. It was very difficult to detect them before you entered the programme, and to a certain extent the cyber junkies and hackers took pot luck with them, though to most of the experienced ones they didn't present much of a danger. Most of them were able to call in the scanning software to capture and quarantine them. Fortunately for me, if you can call being confronted by these worms as fortunate, the Professor was able to call on his old capture and quarantine bot, that bizarre old junk robot that came to my rescue, although he said it did take him a while to remember the installation codes required. He reassured me that Kingly's contact with the worms as he sliced them wouldn't have any lasting effect. While I remained in my virtual cyber suit and connected to Kingly, he had been able to treat and hospitalise Kingly, ensuring that any potential infection had been stopped. Kingly would be fine, which was more than could be said for me. To this day I have an unnatural aversion to worms. Still, Kingly's gene modifications had proved to be spot-on. And while they say practice makes perfect, in this case we decided enough was enough.

VIRTUAL OR
REALITY?

The following week we were summoned once again to the Professor's laboratory. Dr Kirkland had indeed been in touch with Professor Franklin. He had checked that the appropriate gene modifications had been made and tested. Apparently, he had been most encouraged by the edited footage of our performance in the cyber junkyard. He was clearly confident that his illegal scam was going to work beautifully.

Dr Kirkland had indeed found out when our next battle was, and who it was against. We were to battle convincingly; after all, nothing could look staged. But under no circumstances were we to use or show any sign of the new gene modifications in this battle. We had to look convincing, but not that convincing. We mustn't win. Deep down I guess even then we all knew that we couldn't go through with this. We now like to think that it was our indignation at being exploited by an evil toe-rag like Dr Kirkland. However, I'm afraid it might have just been our basic desire to win.

We were sitting glumly in the Professor's office when the door opened. Ann put her head round the door-frame.

"They are here, Professor. Shall I show them in?" she asked.

"Yes, of course. Thank you, Ann."

Who were "they", what was going on? Surely not more trouble? The Professor sat in silence, but strangely he looked more relaxed than I had ever seen him before. Ann quickly returned with the two guests. A tall slim woman with astonishing green eyes. I noticed the resemblance to the Professor. This had to be his granddaughter, and of course the little fair-haired toddler firmly gripping her hand must be Lily. How could such a small innocent thing be at the centre of such a horrible mess? Katie exchanged glances with me and I knew she was thinking the same. What were they doing here? Was Professor Franklin ensuring that we did as we were asked? It's certainly easier to feel sympathetic when you can put a face to a name. I felt like holding up my hands, and confessing there and then that I felt guilty about my rather privileged life.

"Please meet Grace and Lily," said the Professor, pulling up an extra chair facing us. He beckoned to Ann to join us.

"Now, where to begin," he sighed.

I somehow felt we had been here before, the first time the Professor told us about Grace and Lily. That seemed like an age ago.

The Professor told us how he had been to see Grace, and had explained about Dr Kirkland's threats. He was worried that Dr Kirkland would never relinquish his power over him. Grace and Lily would always live in fear of being exposed. It was an impossible situation, and he didn't want to see us dragged into it as well. He said that he should have stood up long before now to Dr Kirkland.

"I am a selfish old man. I couldn't see beyond my beloved Grace and Lily. I so wanted to make things right, but all I've done is escalate the scale of the trouble. I should never have got you involved. If only you hadn't come here." He paused.

If only. It was one of the most powerful wishes out, if only we could make it true. Now I was at it. As my Mum says, what's done is done, you can't change it, you have to move on. Well, we were there now, but I was having serious doubts as to how we could move on.

"What are you going to do, Professor? Surely you aren't going to let that Dr Kirkland tell the gene regulation authorities about Lily, are you?" Katie blurted out, looking horrified.

"Not exactly, my dear. I will do that."

" But you can't. What will happen to them?" Katie was almost off her seat. I would have backed down at that point, but the Professor, who doesn't know Katie as well as we do, smiled and held up a hand for silence.

"No, I am going to do what I should have done years ago on behalf of the innocent children condemned to registration as a clone, some unfortunate slightly-less-than-perfect individuals. It is to my shame that I had to wait until it affected my family before I would do something. I have decided, after speaking with Grace, that I am going to speak out publicly against the programme and the policy for outlawing so-called gene imperfections. I will use archive evidence to show the quality of life before the Gene Proclamation Bill and the Gene Control Centres. We have gone too far, nature should be allowed to have her role, including her mistakes. We can treat the sick, and help the disadvantaged with our medicines and technology. And that is what we should be doing, not seeking the perfect human."

Then Grace spoke.

"Grandfather is right, we should speak out. I was anxious about the danger he was putting himself in, just for me. And besides, we would have had a life of looking over our shoulders, worrying when the awful secret might come out. I'm sorry that you got caught up in this, but we would like to ask you to help us just this once. Dr Kirkland is an evil man, and has managed to hide his criminal activities behind his company Genecon for years. We want to expose him for what he really is. But of course the decision is yours. You don't have to help if you would rather not, you can just walk away now, we would understand."

We briefly exchanged glances. I thought I could judge what the others were thinking, and answered without hesitation.

"Of course we'll help."

"What's the plan?" asked Ed.

Ann, under instructions from the Professor, had been to see her brother, Jake, the one who was an undercover investigator for the Ministry of Mistreatment of Gene Modifications. She told him the whole sorry story and, needless to say, he was very interested. He had been monitoring Dr Kirkland's activities for a while now. He knew that he was involved in the underworld, competition rigging, illegal gambling and live clone battles. But he was a tricky customer to catch. So, based on what Ann had told him, Jake had come up with a plan. This was how it was going to work – well, supposed to work, fingers crossed.

We were to enter the battle, but instead of losing, as Dr Kirkland had told us to, we were to win. Apparently, nobody went against Dr Kirkland's orders, so it was guaranteed that he would go berserk. No doubt he would pay Professor Franklin a visit to find out what was going on. The Professor was then going to claim that it was all our fault, and that because of our inexperience we hadn't realised how powerful our clone had become. Also, he would suggest that it was possible that we hadn't really grasped the seriousness of the situation. Maybe Dr Kirkland needed to remind us that this was not just a game? This was the weak bit, but hopefully Dr Kirkland wouldn't be suspicious about the Professor blaming us. After all, Dr Kirkland would think that the Professor was just looking after his own interests, and his granddaughter's, a trait that Dr Kirkland would easily understand. The intention was to persuade Dr Kirkland to take us all back to his battle arena, on the secret island, to give us a reminder of the real danger we faced if we didn't do as we were told. And that was the easy bit of the plan. Jake was going to kit us out with the latest nanotechnology in surveillance and bugging. And we are not talking ento- mology here. This would enable Jake to get real evidence of Dr Kirkland's illegal activities. But it seemed Jake was wor- ried about Dr Kirkland's connections with people in power, and he didn't want to risk Dr Kirkland squirming his way out of this. So it wasn't good enough just to make sure we had a prime ringside view of the battle arena: Jake intended to transmit live coverage of the illegal battling of real battle clones. He would use us as live transmitters from inside Dr Kirkland's arena, and would monitor the transmission. At an appropriate point Jake would switch this transmission from his viewing port onto the challenge show channel in the cyber cafés. Then, if he was really lucky, he would patch it into one of the 24hr news channels. With this amount of coverage even Dr Kirkland couldn't deny his involvement. This was all well and good as a plan, but there was also the minor point of our safety, carrying out this surveillance in Dr Kirkland's secret hideaway. Apparently, Jake was to use the tracking facility of these nanosurveillance devices to have Dr Kirkland's secret location revealed, and arrange for him to be arrested. Meanwhile, we would be whisked off to safety. That was it, nothing to it. Piece of cake.

THE LAST BATTLE

The day of the battle, the day we had been dreading, arrived. Under normal circumstances at least we would have had the mix of excitement to overcome our nerves. However, all we had was this sinking feeling in the pit of our stomachs that made you feel like throwing up. How could we go through with this? What if it all went horribly wrong? We would all be in big trouble. What an understatement.

Fortunately no one thought anything of our rather solemn demeanour. I guess they put it down to pre-match nerves, maybe they thought we were getting out of our league. We certainly were, but in a very different sort of league. Professor Franklin discussed tactics with us. He made sure that I knew exactly when to use the new gene modifications. They were quite something. I remembered again testing them out in the cyber junkyard. The added power of Kingly's beak was reassuring, and the awesome talons that extended with a twist and a flick were deadly.

We were silent before heading into the gateway, there was nothing that could be said now. I felt my friends' supportive pats on my back, and the whole weight of the problem on my shoulders. What if I failed? What would happen then? I couldn't think like that, I had to let go. I had to let Kingly take control. I felt calm as I transformed. I relaxed, feeling my power. I could do this. Kingly could do it.

I entered the battle arena and did a surveillance swoop looking for my opponent. There he was in the shadows. An oversized rodent, a plague rat called Black Death. Cool name. He was an evil-looking creature, black with piercing red eyes, huge yellow fangs, and a disgusting long, pink, hairless tail which resembled a baby python. Now generally your money would be on a bird of prey up against a rodent. But this was no ordinary rodent, and I was beginning to have doubts. I knew I had to get the upper hand early. I needed confidence from the first strike, but how? I circled low, dipped down teasingly close, then soared back up high. It did the trick. Black Death turned his beady eye on me, slowly curling back the flesh of his mouth to reveal the full horror of his yellow fangs. I could swear he was smiling at me. It was unnerving: clearly the desired effect. With some effort I managed to stop my heart from giving a good impression of a pneumatic drill against my rib cage. It was time, I had to go for it or I would lose the moment. My tactic, if you can call it that, was to go for the tail relatively close to the body so that he couldn't flip himself round and do some damage with his fangs. Once I had him, I was to swing him around and brain him on the nearest rock. Brutal, but effective. This tactic was borrowed from Professor Franklin's knowledge of the laboratory animal houses of his youth, though rather worryingly at that time swinging rats around by their tails to stun them on the edges of benches was considered humane! I did one last sweeping circle, folded in my wings and dived in fast, immediately taking hold of his tail with my talons and then started to ascend. That seemed rather too easy. Suddenly I heard a whipping noise and Black Death's tail swung out and towards me. It coiled tight around me, and like the python it resembled started to squeeze. I thought I was going to burst like some overripe fruit. I couldn't stand the build-up of pressure anymore. Surely it would have to go somewhere. I tried to block out the image of my insides being used to pebble-dash the arena.

I was struggling to maintain my height and my flight path was now very low, exactly what Black Death wanted, encouraging me to loosen my grip and allow him to fall to relative safety. From nowhere I mustered up a last surge of adrenalin, probably a result of fright and flight, rather than fight. But I had to go on. I gained some height and then swivelled my head round and took a wild stab with my beak. I could feel the force of the new gene modification as it met flesh, soft fur-covered flesh: Black Death's body, and not mine. With intense relief I could feel his grip relaxing slightly. That was all I needed, now I was able to move more I could allow my powerful wings to do their job and gain the height I needed. Then, suddenly, I let go of my hold with my talons leaving Black Death to hang on with his tail, he certainly wouldn't let go at this height. With the effortless glide of a well-oiled blade I flicked out my talons and put them into action. It was not a pretty sight, and I guess the game strategists will pull it apart for years to come. Nevertheless, it worked. There was a flurry of fur and feathers being whipped up by a manic pink snake, Black Death's tail. I was not without injury, I felt the first and the second bite from those vicious yellow fangs, but after that, nothing. I could sense by the high-pitched squeals, a primitive animal sound, that I was hitting my target. My razor talons were making black and red ribbons. But still I was unsure whether the warm sticky blood I could feel was his or mine. I felt that I was getting the better of him, but already could feel myself tiring. How long could I keep this up? If I wasn't careful his unnatural stamina would carry him through. I had to finish him soon, before I ran out of energy. Out of the corner of my eye I caught sight of one of the game clones making his way over to join the scrap. What now? I didn't need this. With one last extreme effort I tore myself free from the flailing python, and soared into the sky. Then, letting gravity assist, I took what I knew was my last dive, talons extended. I had become a suicide clone. If I didn't make my target I was cat meat, or should I say rodent meat. It felt like I was falling forever, then my talons met their target. I could feel them sliding through the soft flesh of Black Death's snout and scraping on the bone. With the momentary euphoria of striking my target, and realising I was still alive, I managed to turn around the dive and retreat back into the sky. I left Black Death below, his squeals of pain vibrating in my head. My job was done. He was now left to the mercy of the game clone, and mercy isn't a characteristic high on their gene profile. I had won…just. Not by the skin of my teeth, but by the skin and blood of Black Death, still fresh on my talons.

I am still not sure how I made it back to the portal. I went through and transformed back to myself. I had the strange feeling that this would be the last time that I would be Kingly. I felt drained, empty and sad, like I had lost something precious to me, gone forever. Still, no one had said that it would be easy. We had succeeded with the first part of the plan. Now we had to wait for Dr Kirkland's reaction.

SPIES

We didn't have to wait long. As predicted, Dr Kirkland, in the foulest of moods, paid the Professor a visit the very next day. All went according to plan. Without any difficulty, and not much persuading, Dr Kirkland was convinced that we needed a little reminder of where our loyalties should lie. Basically, we needed showing who was boss. He told the Professor that we would be collected from his laboratory at the end of the week. We were going to be taken on a little trip back to Dr Kirkland's battle arena, to reinforce the importance of our task, and perhaps to gently remind us why we had to get it right. That meant we had just a few days to make preparations.

Ann contacted her brother to let him know that the plan was now in action. We would be taken to the secret location of Dr Kirkland's battle arena at the end of the week. Jake told Ann to bring us over to his place the next evening. That would give him enough time to get the necessary surveillance equipment from work. He said that he couldn't risk us going into his Unit, as a bunch of kids was bound to raise a few eyebrows. It was hardly the sort of place that had hordes of visiting school parties. I was a little disappointed, I was quite looking forward to having a guided tour of one of the top gene spying units. I should have realised that was unrealistic, but then again, given everything that had happened lately, nothing seemed improbable any more.

Ann gave us instructions on how to get to Jake's flat. We were not to go all together, and certainly not at the same time, otherwise we might draw too much attention to ourselves. Besides, Dr Kirkland might be keeping an interested eye on us. I began to feel slightly nervous.

By seven o'clock we had all arrived at Jake's. Ann brought out drinks and snacks, but even we didn't have the stomach to make much of an impression on them. Jake started to explain exactly what surveillance equipment would be used. That was all well and good, until we fully realised that it was actually us who had to do it. The mood changed, the inevitable cloud of doom rested in the room. I felt a shiver pass through my spine. Katie glanced over.

"I'm sure it will all be fine in the end, everything always turns out for the best. Doesn't it?" she said hesitantly, clearly looking for reassurance.

There were a few mumblings, half-agreeing, all of us trying to convince ourselves that it would be just hunky-dory. After all, didn't all stories have a happy ending? I racked my brains, and had to concede that my taste in literature really was on the dark side. Not many happy endings to relate to there. Whatever, there was no turning back now.

Jake continued to brief us on the surveillance equipment he had "borrowed" from his unit. I should explain that these latest surveillance bugs had more in common with the nasty infectious variety than the conventional electronic bugs of earlier decades. These were nanobots, small nanomachines the size of a bacteria that could be injected into the body using a syringe. They were said to be so intelligent, that just injecting a few into the average worker clone would double his or her IQ. Oh well, some upside then. Maybe I would do better in next year's exams. The nanobots which were going to be injected into us were the standard visual-audio bots. Very safe, apparently. The visual bots, known as I-Spys, were programmed to seek out the optic nerve, follow its route, and sit at the fovea on the retina: a perfect viewing position. To ensure full coverage and no blind spots, they were injected in pairs, one for each eye. The audio bots were less sophisticated, and their positioning less critical. Ideally, they would rest just inside the ear canals, using the pinna, that wonderfully fleshy outer ear (well, mine are), as a natural satellite dish. Again, they were injected in pairs for maximum range. I was beginning to feel nervous at playing host to these miniature robots, and just wanted to get the whole process over with.

Jake put on a special pair of eye glasses, with extremely high-powered lenses, to allow him to handle the nanobots. They were stored in small glass vials in some fluorescent liquid. It was as if they were living creatures being nurtured in their own primeval slime. Jake could see me recoil.

"Don't worry, these things are purely mechanical machines. Of course they are designed to function within a host body, so we store them in a medium equivalent to body fluids. Also, this goo helps to protect them from damage," he said with a half-grimace, half-smile.

I wasn't too reassured at this. They still seemed like some alien living creature, deeply scary in my eyes, and that's exactly where they would be. Jake selected the nanobots, prepared the syringe and beckoned for me to step forward. I clenched my fists, teeth and anything else that could be clenched.

"James, you really need to relax or this is going to hurt," said Jake softly.

I stopped holding my breath, and a rush of air came out of my lungs along with some of the tension. At that moment, I felt a sharp prick of the needle, a tiny scratch on my arm, and that was it. I didn't even whimper, unusual for me. The others quickly followed, and before long the task was completed. We were now all impregnated with the little nanobot surveillance machines. I looked around the room but I didn't feel any different. I wasn't seeing any extra images. I listened hard, and thought I could detect extra sounds, and then realised it was just the sound of rushing blood in my ears. I started to relax, maybe it would be okay after all.

With the surveillance bots in place, I felt half-robot, half-James Bond. Just like those old spy movies stored in the archives.

"Hi, I'm James...James Nanobot."

We knew we should be taking this seriously, but we were still scared, and nothing brings out poor jokes more than nerves. We needed to get our act together if we were to pull this off. Jake decided to give us a day settling down with our robotic parasites. Then he called us in to check that the technology was working. It was quite something. Mind you, given that you couldn't switch these things off, I'm glad I didn't get up to anything too embarrassing. We were once again reduced to toilet humour, literally, and this time we had the photographic record complete with sound effects! Jake confirmed that the surveillance bots were working properly, and we were ready for the next phase of the plan. Cue our meeting with Dr Kirkland and his henchmen. We just had to sit and wait for them now.

EXPOSURE

Things were going so smoothly now that I was beginning to feel nervous. What if Dr Kirkland detected our nanobots? What then? Jake had conceded that it was likely that Dr Kirkland had a retina identification profiler, and that this would be programmed to identify the presence of surveillance I-Spys. But, and we hoped this was a very big "but", it was likely to be positioned at the main entrance at adult eye level. We should be able to avoid looking into it directly, given our varying heights, without raising too much suspicion. There have been very few times in my life that I have been thankful for being vertically challenged, and now was one of them. Still, it was going to be a close call for Ed and Luke. Certainly, as a precaution, until we found ourselves safely at the side of the battle arena we were to keep our eyes down, and under no circumstances were we to look up at gateways or doorways, the most likely positions for other profilers. That shouldn't be a problem. Dr Kirkland and his henchmen would just assume that we were all scared. A reasonable assumption under the circumstances, and pretty close to the mark.

As before, we were hustled into the secure travel pod, and then escorted to the secret island location by Dr Kirkland's henchmen. They certainly hadn't acquired any more manners since our last meeting. The bleak volcanic outcrop looked just as grim on second viewing, and the black dust cloud blowing around made the scene seem even more post-holocaust than before. I could detect Katie shivering next to me, and it was not just the cold.

"Welcome my young battlers. You clearly have a natural talent for this, or perhaps are even more stupid than I credited. I will put your little misdemeanour down to a killer winner's instinct. I can identify with an inability to lose. An admirable talent when used appropriately. But you need to know that you never, and I mean never, disobey me. You have cost me dearly for that little escapade. I think you should have a glimpse at how nasty it can really get. Then we will talk about what you can do for me next. I take it that the eagle clone is duly repaired, and the good Professor is applying himself to the next gene modifications you have earned?" Dr Kirkland was staring straight at me.

I felt his glassy stare boring through me. I was sure he would be able to see the nanobot staring right back. I dropped my gaze to the floor.

"Well?" he snapped, making us all jump.

"Yes, sir," we murmured in unison.

"That's better. Now sit back, relax, and enjoy the show. I think you could learn one or two things from this. Dart! Where is that slimy toad? Some drinks here, now."

I could swear that Dart muttered, "Frog actually, sssir," as he moved away.

The battle was about to begin. It was Tri-Killer Knockout. Three battle clones were released into the arena, and were to battle to the death. The winner was the battle clone who placed his chosen weapon, along with a severed body part from each of the losing clones, in the designated holding place, which was an elevated platform located on the top of the highest rock in the arena. It stood out like a beacon. This was a bit like knights of old brandishing standards bearing their coats of arms, but altogether more gruesome. We could tell from the monitor screens that the betting was frantic, large sums of money were being placed on favourite battle clones to win. To make things more interesting, there was a coveted prize for a full-strike kill. For this, heads of the losers had to be mounted on spikes on the platform, but they had to be intact. We were told all this by Dr Kirkland. Apparently, the last time a full strike was completed was over two years ago, but there was a lot of excitement today because a new and very promising battle clone, Silver Claw, was expected to succeed. I could feel the tension in the room, but for once it wasn't just from us. However, I didn't think that it was just the excitement and tension of the forthcoming battle. There was something else, but I couldn't put my finger on it.

The battle clones were deeply scary. A sort of cross between supernatural monsters and deformed comic-book heroes. They had so many modifications it was barely possible to recognise the human clone beneath. They were allowed their one chosen weapon, in addition to the ones that were a fixed part of them. This weapon could be anything apart from any form of firing weapon, so this excluded weapons from guns to flame-throwers and rocket-launchers. Despite these constraints, there was a gruesome array of weapons on display. One resembled a colossal mace with multiple balls of hooked spikes, another was a multi-ended sort of trident, a duodecadent at least, with spiked rosettes at the end of each point. The last weapon in the arena was a slim double-edged blade, almost two metres in length and held like a traditional karate bo, the wooden staff used in martial arts. This was the weapon of choice for Silver Claw, the favourite for the full-strike kill. I really didn't want to see him hack off any heads with that. I wanted to close my eyes as the fighting began, but knew that I needed to keep them open for the I-Spy nanobot. The only way I could get through this was by pretending that I was watching a ridiculous horror film, so absurd and extreme in its violence that it couldn't be true. Maybe Dr Kirkland was playing a sick joke on us and this really was a virtual contest. Unfortunately, I knew this not to be the case. Those screams were for real, but how was Jake going to patch this in to the cyber network, and convince the people watching that it was for real? I hadn't really thought about that before. I guess I had assumed that it would be obvious. At that moment, however, there was a commotion behind us.

Dart appeared to be at the centre of some sort of fight. I caught sight of what I thought was a knife being wrestled out of his hand by Dr Kirkland's henchmen. What on earth was going on? Had Dart had enough of the insults? A bit of an extreme reaction, even so. As I was pondering this, the door of the watching gallery burst open and in poured more clones, spilling out in all directions along the gallery. The scene resembled the invasion of flies over a rotting corpse. I was petrified, the battle clones below were scary in the extreme but these clones were grotesque and close up. They were clearly the result of gene modifications that had gone wrong. It was like the opening of a low budget horror film.

Dart was clearly in command. He was shouting out orders while struggling with the henchmen. Of course he wasn't going to overpower them alone, but soon they were surrounded by a sea of freak clones. I could see the hench-men flinch visibly as the clones closed in under Dart's instructions. I could sense the others recoiling next to me. The gallery was beginning to feel a little overcrowded now with the number of clones that had descended, and the combined stench of bodies and foul breath was making me overcome with nausea. But, as I stood there and watched them, I gradually grew accustomed to the deformities and realised that they were not scary, just sad. I had a feeling that this was going to be even better than our original plan to trap Dr Kirkland. I wasn't disappointed.

Slowly the skirmishes died down, the room was now secure and in the hands of Dart and his cronies. The henchmen, looking somewhat diminished in size, were being held fast in a corner of the gallery. Dart stepped forward and faced a rather white-looking Dr Kirkland. At first I thought he was white with rage, and then realised that he was white with fear. My heart gave an unexpected skip for joy. But not for long. Suddenly Dr Kirkland grabbed Katie, who was sitting next to him and, holding her tightly, pushed her in front.

"Don't move any closer, or try anything silly. If you do the girl gets hurt first," shouted Dr Kirkland.

"Do you really think I care about these over-privileged brats? One less would do us all a favour," said Dart, continuing to move forward.

This was certainly taking a turn for the worse. Katie looked terrified. She just stayed rigid, perfectly still. I wanted to do something, but I was useless, just some stupid kid. I felt worthless. Where was Jake? Was he receiving all of this? Did he know where we were, and more importantly, would anyone get here before it was too late? Behind us in the arena we could still hear the screams of the battle clones, and the bloodthirsty roar from the spectators.

"You won't get away with this, Dart. What is it you and your mutant friends want? A nice cosy place in society? I don't think so. You freaks are never going to be accepted outside of the underworld. You are too embarrassing, a bitter reminder to everyone of just how horribly barbaric this whole world has become. Anything less than perfect is not acceptable. Sorry if I am hurting your feelings. Did you think you could just walk out of here, find the girl of your dreams, get married and acquire a breeding certificate? Most of you freaks are sterile anyway, you will soon die out. Ironic that you would need the technology that created you, that you hate so much, to have children." Dr Kirkland started laughing, the eerie laugh of the unhinged madman in movies.

"We might not look quite so perfect, but there is nothing wrong with our brains," Dart replied. "We know we cannot change things overnight, but we are tired of being your underclass. It is time you tried living as an illegal clone, not even recognised as existing. There are a lot more willing to join us than you think. I have even managed to turn the majority of the battle clones. Now, they would be an interesting force out on the streets. The trouble is, I'm not sure I could control them. I wouldn't like to be responsible for their actions." A faint smile hovered over Dart's lips as he spoke. He was enjoying this.

"So what do you want?" demanded Dr Kirkland.

"Well, we have two possibilities. We use you as our personal campaigner and get you to put our case to the authorities, though I suspect that is a little naïve, and in the land of fairy tales. Besides, you aren't exactly a model citizen. Who would listen to you? The second, and altogether my favourite option, is that we take over the underground world and this secret location. From here we would be able to plan our final integration, and move into society. There are many more of us less-privileged individuals out there than you may think. The authorities haven't quite got the balance right; the problem of having the power in the hands of a small, but undoubtedly perfectly formed, élite few."

Dart paused for effect, before continuing. "You have no choice, Kirkland. Rather like you gave us no choice. We will keep you here as hostage, and I think there may be a few interesting plans for some gene modifications. We hadn't intended to take any others, but these extra guinea pigs might come in handy," he said, turning to look at us. "So let the girl go, and don't waste any more of our time," he snapped. "I am now starting to lose patience."

Dr Kirkland slowly released his grip on Katie, and slumped dejectedly back in his chair. By coincidence there was a massive roar from the arena. I turned to see Silver Claw standing triumphantly on top of the rocks with two severed heads held up high. He had got the full strike.

What happened next was all a bit of a blur. It all happened so fast, and there was a lot of confusion. Jake had managed to patch into the cyber network and very quickly had got our live coverage into the news channel. In no time, the ether was jammed with mails. Clearly, the news station knew nothing about this, but Jake had primed senior colleagues and soon everything was working like clockwork. The news channel was briefed, and they were able to put out a message while continuing to broadcast. This was definitely shock and awe territory, and the public was gripped.

All this time our location was being tracked and an anti-gene-mutant terrorist squad was being sent in. For the second time in what seemed like a very short while the doors to the gallery burst open, only this time uniformed military swarmed in. I remember thinking this place is getting seriously overcrowded, and physically gasping for air, but maybe that was just fear. Instinctively I dived for the floor, almost colliding with Ed and Luke. I looked around for Katie. She had run for the doors, as far away from Dr Kirkland as possible. How she didn't get hurt, I don't know. Almost as soon as the military entered they started shooting, laser beams bouncing across the gallery. The stench of burning flesh made me gag and the screams seemed to reverberate around my brain. Like the others I struggled to stay conscious. The killing appeared indiscriminate; there were mutant clones and Kirkland's henchmen dropping like flies. I guess if I had been thinking more I would have kept watching and so ensured that the scene was recorded, but I had no inclination to keep my head up in that battle arena. Likewise I am sure the anti-gene-mutant terrorist squad were glad not to have the full glory of their massacre broadcast. Not quite the clean contain-and-control mission they prided themselves on, just straightforward elimination, the usual cleansing of mutants. I am sure the survivors were the ones on the floor at the bottom of the pile, seeking refuge among the dead, which is where we found ourselves.

I am not sure how much is confused and how much is deliberately blocked out. I feel that we had a glimpse of the darker side of existence that day: whether you call it hell or a living nightmare, words can barely describe it. But it is something I certainly don't want ever to face again. It will take a long time for the memories to fade and the psychological scars to heal. I still can't stand being in crowded places, and Katie gets panicky when approached from behind. Still, we have a lot to be thankful for; we were extremely lucky that we survived the ordeal. And although that was more or less the end of the story for us, in many ways it was the beginning for many others.

A BETTER SOCIETY

The rest isn't really our story, but I feel quite proud that we helped put some of this in place, even if it was by accident. I suspect that by the time I am an old man I will bore my grandchildren with the tale of how I helped to change society. And hopefully there should be no question by then of whether I am allowed to have my own grandchildren!

As you would expect there was public outrage when our live coverage of the underworld was broadcast. As ever, there were groups of people who would not accept it, and said that was what you expected with clones, conveniently forgetting that Dr Kirkland, the instigator of all this, was one of their so-called perfect élite. They called for tighter regulations and the culling of rogue clones, in particular the mutant gene clones like Dart and his cronies, though from what I saw the anti-gene-mutant terrorist squad had already wiped out quite a few without a second thought. Where was the public outcry there? Fortunately the majority of people could see the flaws in our society and what we had become. People started talking nostalgically of the past, family traits, characteristics that had been modified out. For a while my quirky ears became trendy, a throwback to ancestors. A stand against genetic perfection. It even became acceptable to openly question where we were going as a race, to ask what we had really gained from striving for human perfection. There was no question that in medicine and technology we had achieved beyond what anyone could have dreamt about centuries ago. We were in a position to play God, but we were still human, and we all know human nature is to make mistakes.

However, no change happens overnight. It takes time and a lot of debate. In the meantime what happened to Grace and Lily? After all, they were the precipitating factor in all this. Well, I'm afraid that there were no immediate fairytale endings. Professor Franklin did go to the gene regulation authority, along with Grace and Lily, and informed them of what had happened. It was extraordinary, the amount of public support they had. Not for many years had so many people gathered for a public demonstration. Still, the authorities had no choice under current law but to register Lily as a clone and revoke Grace's breeding licence. Despite this, which Professor Franklin and Grace saw as a necessary setback to go forward, they were happy, and became the driving force behind a movement campaigning for the rights of clones and the reform of the breeding laws. In fact, I heard that Grace is now expecting another child, bypassing the authorities and gene centres like many others. While this is technically illegal, the authorities are turning a blind eye with the expectation of reforms in the near future. It is easy to accept now that perfection is a dangerous goal and a cruel one.

Professor Franklin became a vigorous campaigner and dedicated the rest of his life to helping the mutant gene clones like Dart. After initial hostility they formed an unusual alliance. Fortunately, Dart had not been seriously injured in the raid and he became the Professor's assistant, helping him move in the circle of the gene mutants who had remained hidden in their dangerous underworld. The Professor was actually happier than he had ever been, using his gene modification skills to help these poor people. In some way, I guess he was paying back for his role in striving for human perfection that partly led to this mess.

There is one important person that I mustn't forget: Kingly. What became of our own creation, our animal clone? Needless to say the competition was abandoned and the virtual reality gaming laws were tightened up. All minors under eighteen were no longer allowed to access the games that had become so popular and part of our culture. I can see where this comes from, but feel that this is an over-reaction. After all, there have been many times in history where computer games have been blamed for things going wrong in society and never with any concrete proof. But then I am a teenage boy obsessed with computers. The worst thing was that the virtual clones created for the game were to be condemned, their computer programming irrevocably destroyed by a lethal virus injection. I couldn't do it; I couldn't destroy what had increasingly become part of me. Destroying Kingly felt like killing a member of my family, my twin. I left the task to Professor Franklin. A part of me hopes that he, too, couldn't do it and that he managed to consign Kingly to one of the defunct computer arenas, effectively setting him free into the wild. At least he would have a fighting chance there. I guess I will never know.

What of us? Well, we have grown up in many ways. It would sound so pathetic to say that we were all the better because of our experience. At times I really wish I hadn't had to go through all that, but then I have those wistful moments remembering Kingly. Secretly, I miss my flights as him. If it had all stayed within the confines of the game it would have been fun. It is only when games and reality get mixed up that it goes horribly wrong. I'm sorry, you were just as much a victim as everyone else, Kingly…goodbye my friend, I won't forget you.